'This book is to be welcomed as [...] is presented as an introduction to important and prolific thinkers in p[...] But it takes us on a journey through Donald Meltzer's work in a really intelligent way, guided by the author and her in-depth knowledge.

The book will allow readers to recreate the atmosphere of the clinical seminars and supervisions shared with Donald Meltzer. His optimism about the human spirit holds all of us who choose to engage in the task of holding "the most interesting conversation in the world" in the consulting room and in the different settings we inhabit.'

Virginia Ungar, M.D., International Psychoanalytical Association (IPA) President

'This is an excellently structured and immensely readable book, which is bound to whet the appetite to read Donald Meltzer's original work.

It is no easy task to introduce an *oeuvre* of eight books and a large collection of essays, conference talks and clinical papers into a 40,000-word volume, but Meg Harris Williams has succeeded in that elegantly and rigorously. She presents Meltzer's understanding of his teachers: Freud, Klein, Money-Kyrle and Bion, crucially pinpointing the aspects of their theories that had stimulated his original thinking.

Williams skilfully manages to serve two masters: the theoreticians, who will be impressed by her academic style, and the clinicians, who will relish the quoted clinical examples. The latter show her deep appreciation and respect for Meltzer, who maintained that any psychoanalytic theory must be conceived, gestated and born in the consulting room.'

Irene Freeden, Training and Supervising Psychoanalyst, British Psychoanalytic Association

'Meg Harris Williams has managed to offer us more than just an introduction to Meltzer's *oeuvre*. This book visits almost each milepost of Meltzer's evolution as an analytic original thinker. She brings his concepts back in her own clarifying words and illustrates them with generous citations from Meltzer's writings. It reads like a *pas-de-deux* between explanation and citation, thus both inspiring the reader's thoughts as well as stimulating (healthy) curiosity which will lead many to study Meltzer's books and articles. For the reader already familiar with Meltzer's writings, it will offer a fresh look into them, and a very enjoyable one.

Williams pays homage to Meltzer who developed, enriched and applied the works of Freud, Klein and Bion. This rather short book is a *délicatesse* to savor and let "dissolve in your mind".'
Robert Oelsner, **M.D.**, Psychoanalyst FIPA, Psychoanalytic Institute of Northern California

Donald Meltzer

In this intelligent and insightful work, Meg Harris Williams presents a clear and readable introduction to the works of influential psychoanalyst Donald Meltzer. The book covers Meltzer's ideas on key themes including sexuality, dreams, psychosis, perversion and aesthetics, and his work with both children and adults.

This book focuses especially on Meltzer's views on the nature of psychoanalysis itself, as an investigative method conducted by the cooperation between two people. His intuitive understanding of dreams is underscored by a scholarly interest in philosophy and linguistics. The book will give readers a window into Meltzer's clinical seminars and supervisions, as well as a comprehensive overview of his published work, all thoughtfully brought together by someone who worked with Meltzer for many years.

Bringing Meltzer's ideas into contemporary context, this fresh approach to his work makes his rich and complex theories about our inner world accessible to all. Part of the *Routledge Introductions to Contemporary Psychoanalysis* series, this book will be of great importance to psychoanalysts, clinicians and scholars familiar with Meltzer's ideas, as well as those seeking an introduction to his work.

Meg Harris Williams is a literary scholar and former analysand of Meltzer. She was formerly a lecturer for the Psychoanalytic Studies MA course at the Tavistock and Portman Trust, London.

Routledge Introductions to Contemporary Psychoanalysis

Aner Govrin
Series Editor

Tair Caspi
Associate Editor

Books in the Routledge Introductions to Contemporary Psychoanalysis series will serve as concise introductions dedicated to influential concepts, theories, leading figures and techniques in psychoanalysis.

The length of each book is fixed at 40,000 words.

The series books are designed to be easily accessible so as to provide informative answers in various areas of psychoanalytic thought. Each book will provide updated ideas on topics relevant to contemporary psychoanalysis – from the unconscious and dreams, projective identification and eating disorders, through neuropsychoanalysis, colonialism and spiritual-sensitive psychoanalysis. Books will also be dedicated to prominent figures in the field, such as Melanie Klein, Jacques Lacan, Sándor Ferenczi, Otto Kernberg and Michael Eigen.

Not serving solely as an introduction for beginners, the purpose of the series is to offer compendia of information on particular topics within different psychoanalytic schools. We ask authors to review a topic but also address the readers with their own personal views and contribution to the specific chosen field. Books will make intricate ideas comprehensible without compromising their complexity.

We aim to make contemporary psychoanalysis more accessible to both clinicians and the general educated public.

Published titles

Donald Meltzer
A Contemporary Introduction
By Meg Harris Williams

Donald Meltzer

A Contemporary Introduction

Meg Harris Williams

LONDON AND NEW YORK

Cover image © Michal Heiman, Asylum 1855–2020, The Sleeper
(video, psychoanalytic sofa and Plate 34), exhibition view,
Herzliya Museum of Contemporary Art, 2017

First published 2022
by Routledge
2 Park Square, Milton Park, Abingdon, Oxon OX14 4RN

and by Routledge
605 Third Avenue, New York, NY 10158

Routledge is an imprint of the Taylor & Francis Group, an informa business

© 2022 Meg Harris Williams

The right of Meg Harris Williams to be identified as author of this work has been asserted by her in accordance with sections 77 and 78 of the Copyright, Designs and Patents Act 1988.

All rights reserved. No part of this book may be reprinted or reproduced or utilised in any form or by any electronic, mechanical or other means, now known or hereafter invented, including photocopying and recording, or in any information storage or retrieval system, without permission in writing from the publishers.

Trademark notice: Product or corporate names may be trademarks or registered trademarks, and are used only for identification and explanation without intent to infringe.

British Library Cataloguing-in-Publication Data
A catalogue record for this book is available from the British Library

Library of Congress Cataloging-in-Publication Data
Library of Congress Control Number: 2021949590

ISBN: 978-0-367-42222-6 (hbk)
ISBN: 978-0-367-42223-3 (pbk)
ISBN: 978-0-367-82282-8 (ebk)

DOI: 10.4324/9780367822828

Typeset in Times New Roman
by Newgen Publishing UK

Contents

Foreword by Virginia Ungar   ix

Introduction: A picture of the inner world   1

PART I
The psychoanalytic model of the mind   5

1   The Kleinian development   7
     Freud's neurophysiological model 8
     Klein's spatial inner world 11
     Bion and the post-Kleinian model 15
     Evolutionary ethics (Money-Kyrle) 18

2   Dream life and symbol formation   21
     Revising the Freudian theory 22
     An aesthetic theory of dreams 24
     Symbol formation 27

3   An expanded view of identification   31
     Projective identification 31
     Introjective identification 33
     Mind-to-mind and container–contained 36
     Adhesive identification 38

4 Aesthetic conflict *Interest 47* *The prenatal aesthetic 50*	45
5 The Claustrum *The three chambers of the Claustrum 60* *The delusional system 68*	57
6 Sexuality and creativity *Infantile sexual states of mind 72* *Adolescence 74* *The perversions and addictions 76* *Creativity and the adult state of mind 77*	70

PART II
Life in the consulting room   83

7 The aesthetics of the process *The setting and the task 91* *The natural history of the process 94*	85
8 Transference and countertransference *The preformed transference 104* *Observation and the countertransference dream 107* *Dream interpretation 110* *A dream sequence to illustrate misconception 113*	102
9 Technique *Music and interpretative exploration 119* *Technical problems of the Claustrum 123* *Supervision as a dimension of clinical work 129*	118
10 Beyond the consulting room *Psychoanalysis as a thing-in-itself 135* *Psychoanalysis and the arts 138* *The child in the family in the community 143*	134
Glossary of Meltzerian concepts	151
Bibliography	153
Index	156

Foreword

This book is to be welcomed as both timely and necessary. It is presented as an introduction to the work of one of the most important and prolific thinkers in psychoanalysis of recent times. But it is a book that takes us on a journey through Donald Meltzer's work in a really intelligent way, guided by the author and her in-depth knowledge.

Meg Harris Williams does a truly remarkable job of bringing together a whole lifetime's writings of a psychanalyst and profound thinker, who always started out from clinical work to produce theory of a psychoanalysis alive and open to new evidence and findings. Only someone who worked with him for so many years and who witnessed his ideas as they grew closer to art and its various expressions, mainly literature and aesthetics, could have achieved this.

This book will allow readers to recreate the atmosphere of the clinical seminars and supervisions shared with Donald Meltzer. He used to squint his eyes, and we would think that he was sleeping, but he was actually connecting with his own 'picture of the inner world', which emerged from his great capacity for reverie and his incomparable observation skills. From time to time, he would describe this process to the group of analysts and psychotherapists who followed him with great admiration in this conversation, as 'the most interesting' at that time. This was how he believed psychoanalysis should be transmitted, in the form of an atelier. And he was right. The passion for something that is more than just a task can only be conveyed in a personal way. It is about holding the analytical attitude in the consulting room and outside of it. It is about believing in the possibility for development of a child, a patient, a society and the world, in spite of all the anti-thinking and anti-truth forces that seem to prevail in the world of banality.

This optimism about the human spirit, which Donald Meltzer maintained until the end, holds all of us who choose to engage in the task of holding 'the most interesting conversation in the world' in the consulting room and in the different settings we inhabit.

Virginia Ungar, M.D.
International Psychoanalytical Association (IPA) President

Introduction
A picture of the inner world

Donald Meltzer (1922–2004) was one of the most influential London Kleinians and a renowned international teacher, though also a controversial one. His books are all clinically based and all original in their interpretation or extension of post-Kleinian theory. They have been published in many languages and continue to be translated into others. This book introduces readers to his ideas on sexuality, dream life, psychosis and perversion, autism and aesthetics; and on the nature of psychoanalysis itself as an artistic mode of cooperation between two people or rather their 'internal objects', with the aim not of normalising but of 'rescuing the lost children of the personality'. He worked with both children and adults and was innovative in the treatment of autistic children. In addition, Meltzer's longstanding and well-informed interest in the philosophy of language and aesthetics illuminated for him the aesthetic nature of the psychoanalytic method and of the struggle for mental health. This introduction to his work can be considered as 'a picture of the inner world', in honour of Roger Money-Kyrle's book *Man's Picture of his World*, whose title Meltzer said had 'got it right'. He, too, saw the crucial problem in terms of the individual's picture of reality.

Meltzer was born in New York and studied medicine at Yale. After practising as a psychiatrist specialising in children and families, he moved to England in 1953 to have analysis with Melanie Klein; he described this as 'a wild ride' (he was a great horse-lover). He became an enthusiastic British citizen, though resented losing his American citizenship. For years he was a training member of the British Society, though later fell out with them over questions of training, as he was against the quest for respectability and believed in an 'atelier system' which facilitated supervised self-selection. Not only this: his first two books, *The Psychoanalytical Process* (1967) and *Sexual States of Mind* (1973), created a furore in the Society owing to their ideas about psychoanalysis itself; it was a period when, after Klein's death, dreams and the Kleinian language of 'part-objects' were going out of fashion. For Meltzer, this concrete, pictorial view of the inner world was what made psychoanalysis real and interesting: 'the dream is my landscape', he said. His great love was immersion in clinical work, his own or that of students, which he said was the only place he was truly imaginative – not in his books. Meltzer's own teaching came to focus on the Tavistock Clinic where he worked closely with Esther Bick and Martha Harris on the Child Psychotherapy programme, which strove to put into practice Bion's principle of 'learning from experience', on supervisions, and on teaching abroad, to individuals and groups of all sizes. Mainly with Harris (whom he married after her husband's death) he taught regularly in many European countries, especially Italy, France and Spain, and in Scandinavia and North and South America.

Although Meltzer spent many years working with difficult schizophrenic and autistic patients, he increasingly viewed normal development as more complex than psychopathology, and thought that analysts should pay more attention to the 'wealth of evidence' about this that featured in the consulting room. His absorption of the ideas of Wilfred Bion gave substance to this conviction, since it became clear why normal development was so difficult: it involved learning to think, and this was a sophisticated process still embryonic in terms of human evolution. Work with autistic children, in particular, expanded the horizons of symbol formation and clarified retreat from aesthetic conflict. It also became clear why psychoanalysis, as a new method, needed to link hands with the arts and theologies which for centuries had been investigating the mysteries of the human mind.

Meltzer's definition of psychoanalysis was 'working with the transference', whether under the banner of psychoanalysis or of psychotherapy, or indeed it could take place in other situations. He admired craftsmanship in all fields, the marriage of intellectual problem-solving with practical skill. The craft of psychoanalysis he saw as an art-science in its very early stages, pursuing a logical development in which theory and observation proceeded in tandem, one gradually refining the other. He called this incremental expansion of the picture of the inner world 'the most interesting conversation in the world': one that, as with the alchemists, could eventually lead to 'a science of great grandeur'.

On a personal level his outlook was all-inclusive; he made it an item of credo to trust everyone, until proved otherwise – resulting in a few transparent defraudments which annoyed his family but not him; and also in some wounding of those who inexplicably found they were no longer trusted. He made lasting friendships with many of his ex-patients and supervisees, though he accepted that this was not the inevitable epilogue to a transference relationship. Socially, he enjoyed theatre, tennis, skiing, red wine and good home-cooked food. He admired his father for treating with equanimity both the making of a fortune and the loss of it. Like many Americans of his era, he was charmed by the English language and accent and lamented the decline of good grammar. But he was allergic to delusions of grandeur and to indications of snobbery of any type, including the inverted.

Don Meltzer was a powerful and sometimes difficult personality; but he was hospitable, gently humorous and infinitely patient with anyone who genuinely sought his help or who was trying to do the work which he judged the most difficult and most rewarding in the world. That is, apart from being an artist or a musician, which he regarded with awe. He had an interest in architecture (his father was a builder) and enjoyed designing home improvements. With regard to the natural world, he enjoyed cultivating fruit and vegetables and other physical work in the garden, and drank in the beauty of forests and fertile landscapes (he disliked barrenness, however spectacular). He was happy to swim in a cold mountain river but had no sea-legs. He liked dogs and worshipped horses, some of whom certainly retained a place in his internal pantheon. Although he confessed he was always a little depressed owing to the state of the world, he disapproved of pessimism, thinking it an expression of unconscious illwill, and advocated being 'adamantly cheerful' in adverse circumstances. Ultimately, and above all, he advocated like Polonius being true to yourself, which means being true to your internal objects, the 'saints and angels of psychic reality' – those 'aspects of your own personality which contain the aspects of genius that you can only aspire to' ('Thought disorder', 2005b, p. 428).

Part I

The psychoanalytic model of the mind

Chapter 1
The Kleinian development

Meltzer saw psychoanalysis as an art-science. He differentiated between psychoanalytic theory and the psychoanalytic model of the mind that was in use in clinical practice, which he regarded as far more complex and harder to describe, and also as transcending schools of psychoanalysis and their institutional bodies. In his view, all clinical relationships conducted on a transference basis came under the umbrella of psychoanalytic work. Describing the model that is being used has implications for the psychoanalytic method, advancing its subtlety and potential, making psychic movements more observable, and this in turn expands the model, contributing incrementally to the development of a psychoanalytic body of knowledge. For Meltzer, the progressive features of the model were best illuminated by the Kleinian line of advance: beginning with Freud's discovery of the transference and moving through Klein's (and Abraham's) exploration of children's phantasy life to Bion's new perspective on thinking and the relevance of psychoanalysis as a Kantian 'thing in itself'.

Almost without exception, Meltzer's books and papers begin with a summary of the history of this model of the mind, with particular relevance to the topic in hand – be this dreams, sexuality, transference, psychosis, etc. When he published *The Kleinian Development* (1978), a transcript of lectures given to Tavistock

DOI: 10.4324/9780367822828-3

psychotherapy students in the mid-1970s, he was not interested in the politics of psychoanalytic history but in the development of its working method and model of the mind. Science, he said, is 'truly rational in its history': 'To borrow an image from Freud's early writing: in the history of psychoanalysis revelations or discoveries ... adhere to a chain of logically necessary propositions as garlands of flowers wind about a wire' ([1978] 2018, vol. 1, p. 1). His personal study of psychoanalytic history focuses on this logical necessity: what are the features of Freud's model that endure, not as points of debate or argument but as the legacy of his clinical work? How is Klein's model founded on Freud's and how does it depart from it, as a result of her clinical work? Meltzer has a vivid logical and pictorial scheme encompassing the various flowers that make up the garland of the psychoanalytic model. In tracing its evolution, he is constantly aware of the 'wealth of evidence regarding psychic health and growth' gained from the consulting room, often overlooked owing to the concentration on pathological features, yet essential to the completeness of the model.

Freud's neurophysiological model

Meltzer describes Freud's model as essentially neurophysiological; Klein's as geographic-theological; and Bion's as epistemological. Freud was dealing with impulse life and its gratification or frustration; Klein with the baby's relation to the mother who embodies, initially, 'the world'; Bion with the meaning of emotional experiences, as distinct from instinctual impulses:

> If Freud's world is one of creatures seeking surcease from the constant bombardment of stimuli from inside and out, a world of higher animals, and Melanie Klein's world in one of holy babes in holy families plagued by the devils of split-off death

instinct, Bion's world is one of the questing mind seeking the absolute truth with inadequate equipment.

([1978] 2018, vol. 3, p. 123)

Meltzer was an erudite Freud scholar and always maintained his interest, but he did not think Freud's early neurophysiological model was realistic or genuinely scientific. Reviewing the beginnings of psychoanalysis, Meltzer found the work of Freud's mentor Breuer more impressive: 'Jokingly one may say that the inventor of psychoanalysis was Anna O. with her "talking cure" and "chimney sweeping"' ([1978] 2018, vol. 1, p. 15). But Freud showed himself a 'great man' when he was able to learn from the experience of being laughed at by a child named Dora. The Freud Meltzer really admired was the clinician, 'an artist at work', who was prepared to be surprised by his own patients: 'for Dora hurt Freud as Anna O. frightened Breuer' (p. 16); it was this open curiosity that resulted in the discovery of the transference and the psychoanalytic method proper. Indeed Meltzer always saw psychoanalysis as 'a collaborative investigation by patient and analyst' in which the patient is the main investigator; and 'the greatest of the "patients" would be the fellow whom Freud analysed in his self-analysis' (p. 16). The transference, however, was seen by Freud, and for a long time after, as retrospective in its significance, with the patient suffering from reminiscences, rather than (as in modern psychoanalysis) a phenomenon of the present emotional contact.

Meltzer compares the evolution of Freud's thought to 'a country that underwent two revolutions: the first being the fall of the theory of hysteria, and the second being the overthrow of the theory of the libido in the 1920s and its substitution by the structural theory' (Meltzer & Harris [2011] 2018, p. 103). He describes this ultimate model – the structural one of ego, id and superego – as postulating an 'undifferentiated mass of psychic energy, both creative and destructive' (the id), from which the ego evolves with a capacity for the perception of psychic qualities defined as 'consciousness', that seeks to establish an active equilibrium in the world despite having to 'serve three masters'. The primary aim is to minimise tension by seeking a balance or compromise:

> But to the complexities inherent in the conflict of life and death instincts there is added the task of serving or evading the demands of the real world and of an internal institution, the super-ego derived from childhood relation to parents and variously modified by later experiences with figures of dependence, authority and admiration. In this plight, 'serving three masters', the ego resorts to various devices: interposing thought between impulse and action; actions to modify external reality; hallucinatory wish fulfilment and the mechanisms of defence.
> (Meltzer [1978] 2018, vol. 3, p. 120)

Although a structural model rather than a neurophysiological one, it is still based on the idea of trying to balance the demands of conflicting parts of the personality and avoid the discomfort of an imbalance; Meltzer found it a rather pessimistic picture of 'having to outwit the id, outwit the superego, and outwit the community in order to get a little gratification' ([1989] 2021, p. 23). In general, Freud's theoretical model, in Meltzer's view, differs from that of the intuitive and empathic clinician who said he was 'writing novels' about patients he saw as real people, including himself. Freud he saw as a split genius:

> Freud himself seemed to be split between the artist-clinician, the obsessional theoretician, and the political 'Moses figure' who aspired to lead a prestigious intellectual movement, free from 'deviants'.
> ([1978] 2018, vol. 1, p. 66)

Klein's spatial inner world

By contrast, Melanie Klein's model is not based on an explanatory causal system but is 'a description of the geography of phantasy life' in which parts of the self and objects communicate in a 'theatre for the generating of meaning' – an inner world. Phantasies are transactions actually taking place in the inner world, not reminiscences. Meltzer said Klein described far more than she theorised. Explicitly she followed Freud and did not consider herself a deviant. But disapproval was inevitable, as her observations of the drama of the inner world, as manifest in children's play and adult phantasy, impelled her to deal in genuine internal object relations rather than in libido and sublimations. This model emphasises development rather than equilibrium. Its foundation is the construction of an inner world, which commences shortly after birth through the baby's relation to the mother (initially the breast, as part-object):

> By means of splitting the self and object into good and bad, and by phantasies of introjection and projective identification, implemented by a sense of omnipotence, the baby constructs from its gratifying and frustrating experiences an internal world of objects and parts of the self in which its unconscious phantasies and dreams manipulate the meaning and emotional significance of its experiences.
>
> ([1978] 2018, vol. 3, p. 20)

Splitting and idealisation of self and object were seen by Klein to be the first definitive step in healthy development, to which Meltzer adds the philosophical affirmation of Roger Money-Kyrle, describing 'the inner logical necessity of development' from the cognitive point of view ([1975] 2018, p. 226).

This inner world, with its developing capacities, then becomes the basis for construing meaning and hence behaviour in the outside world. Klein postulated the baby's 'epistemophilic instinct' in relation to its mother, initially the mother's body, the prototype for dealing with later experiences, and the focus of both love and hate. Bad or damaged objects, essentially attacked by bad parts of the self, engender persecutory anxieties, defended against by mechanisms such as splitting, projective identification or denial of psychic reality. The developmental goal is to acknowledge and reintegrate split-off parts, thus strengthening the personality, and to establish a trusting dependence upon internal objects through introjective identifications. Gradually this grows into concern for these internal parents, moving beyond simple self-interest. This acceptance of internal reality gives the adult part of the personality more control of its relation with the outside world – more realistic and less projective – while the internal objects take care of the infantile transference and keep it contained. The personality moves from the paranoid-schizoid position (splitting and projecting) to the depressive position, with its implication of ethical values and responsibility in response to the object:

> The paranoid-schizoid and the depressive position are the main economic principles of relations with the *object*. The paranoid-schizoid position is a value system in which the health, security and pleasure of the self dominate, whilst the depressive position is a value system in which the health, security and happiness of the object prevail.
> (Meltzer & Harris [2011] 2018, p. 108)

Meltzer terms it a 'theological' model as the internal objects perform the function of gods in relation to the developing mind; and he stresses that these are real functions, not just metaphors ('as if').

> As the various children of a single family discover eventually that, experientially, they have 'different' parents, so it is that the different parts of the self have different internal objects. For some parts of the self objects are at a partial object level, for others they are invaded and altered by projections; for some

the paternal and maternal are far apart while for others they are combined; for some they are held under omnipotent control, while other parts of the self can give their internal objects their freedom. From this point of view reintegration of the self is contingent upon the reintegration, in a sense the rehabilitation, of the internal objects.

([1992] 2018, p. 58)

This vision of personality development, acquired from work with children, is then extrapolated to form the basis of psychoanalytic work in general, seen as a 'corrective developmental experience':

Under this model psychoanalytical therapy is mainly aimed at making possible a re-experiencing of the essence of the developmental process through the transference, its evolution being facilitated by interpretation. It is essentially a corrective developmental experience in which reintegration of split-off parts of self and objects is facilitated by achievement of the depressive position. But the goodness of this experience may even modify the virulence of the death instinct as it is represented in attitudes of envy and their interference with the development of gratitude and thus of love.

([1978] 2018, vol. 3, p. 121)

The corrective experience is accessed by dipping into a tiny part of the continuous stream of unconscious phantasy that is produced by innate mechanisms of projection and introjection, 'managing a commerce between the spaces of outer and inner world of objects and self'. This stream of unconsciousness exists in both waking and sleeping states, and is highlighted during the transference of the session. Meltzer stresses the spatial qualities of the Kleinian model, saying that:

It is a great advance over Freud in that it provides, by this interaction of mechanisms, a theatre where meaning can be generated (the internal world) and thus makes this arena primary for emotional relations. We see the external world *as,* that is as a reflection of internal relations from the point of view of meaning and significance. There is no such apparatus in Freud's model, the distinction between pleasure and reality principles being so bound to body sensations and gratification of instinctual needs, the alternative to which is hallucinatory wish fulfilment.

([1978] 2018, vol. 3, p. 43)

It is for its spatial qualities that he terms the Kleinian model a 'geographical' one, and in his own theoretical works he details its different terrains and their respective modes of identification, while its essentially 'theological' nature takes the form of the leading role of internal objects in enabling the infant self to develop.

In line with his view of the gradual evolution of Klein's model, Meltzer describes the slight but significant changes in her view of the 'positions':

In the third phase of the use of the 'positions', beginning with writings on mourning and continuing with those on schizoid mechanisms, there is a slow and gradual change. By the time of *Envy and Gratitude* (1957) the entire approach has changed. The paranoid-schizoid and depressive positions start to lose their evolutionary specificity. She no longer describes them as something which occurs at the third month of life and resolves around the time of weaning, but starts to consider them as a type of mental conflict which has its origin around the third month but continues for the entire life of the individual.

([1978] 2018, vol. 2, p. 143)

The depressive position therefore is no longer described as something which is to be overcome, but something which is entered into. The movement between paranoid-schizoid and depressive positions begins to be seen as a continuous oscillation in the sense later delineated sharply by Dr Bion as Ps$\leftrightarrow$D. The concept of love is modified to mean that concern for the wellbeing of the object predominates over concern for the comfort of the self.

This change from a chronological (phase) view of the positions to a continuous oscillation (a phase view) forms the basis for the 'post-Kleinian' model – a designation which Meltzer reluctantly accepted, and indeed, he said that Klein herself was 'the first post-Kleinian' (2005a, p. xii). It is a 'field' conception rather than a 'phase' conception of development, meaning that psychoanalysis too needs to focus on the present moment rather than on the past ([1986] 2018), p. 246).

Bion and the post-Kleinian model

Meltzer says the Kleinian development reads 'like a fairy story':

> Once upon a time there was an Emperor whose name was Freud and his patients defrauded him by clothing him in transference so that he believed that he was good and handsome and wise. But then a child called Dora laughed at him and he realised that he was just naked Freud. But then a great man, Freud, understood that the clothing of the transference had its own psychic reality and that accepting his nakedness beneath it gave him a strange beauty and power to heal his patients' minds. But later on others discovered that wearing this clothing of the transference did really effect some developmental change in wisdom and benevolence (recognition of the countertransference); while failure to remember the nakedness underneath bred grandiosity, complacency, greed.
>
> Still later it was discovered that this recognised fiction of their relationship also enabled both partners to use their minds for thinking to a degree that neither was able to do by himself (Bion). But then it began to become clear that in fact they were not using their minds, their minds were using them. Some time later ...
>
> (Meltzer & Williams [1988] 2018, pp. 23–24)

He saw this development as logical and natural. The Kleinian model is still the solid basis of the 'post-Kleinian': nothing is negated but a new dimension opens up with the work of Bion (also an analysand of Klein). Now it is 'later' and the epistemological dimension has been revealed: the developmental role of the search for knowledge and understanding, not just pleasure or gratification. This goes beyond Freud's two principles of pleasure and reality, which are bound to body sensations and instinctual needs, and beyond Klein's epistemophilic instinct, becoming part of the wider philosophical tradition of the lifelong quest for self-knowledge. As the body needs food, the mind needs truth to survive; love and hate are not enough – we need to know the meaning of our emotions. We do not use our minds, we are used by them, as a potential vehicle for reality; as Bion put it, 'Disguised as fiction, the truth occasionally slips through'.

Meltzer describes the implications of adding Bion to the picture:

> The growth of the mind is not, as in Freud, the natural realisation of innate processes, all going well; nor, like Melanie Klein's, is it a process of complicated unfolding given sufficient nurturing and protection; it is rather seen by Bion as the growth of the capacity for thinking about emotional experiences which enable the individual to learn by becoming a different person with different capabilities from the person of the past.
>
> ([1978] 2018, vol. 3, p. 123)

The pattern of development is not so much corrected as explored. It opens to the unknown – the unknown shape of the new personality. This entails a need to relinquish memory and desire (the already-known shapes, whether set in past or future) and to focus sharply on the present experience and its meaning:

> The life of the individual is in the moment of his being himself having experiences and thinking about them, the past and the

future being hindrances in so far as he is living in them rather than in the present. Nothing described by Freud or Melanie Klein is thus replaced by Bion's model, but would be relegated to row F (scientific deductive system about man as intelligent animal) and row C (the mind's mythology about itself and its origins) respectively.

(p. 123)

Meltzer refers here to Bion's 'Grid' for mapping the development of a thought, inside or outside the psychoanalytic session. Whether or not the boxes of the Grid correspond to the experience of particular analysts or patients, the general picture is clear: that a thought begins with a feeling (initially perhaps not even 'felt', that is, noticed) and progresses through a series of increasingly abstract stages until it becomes satisfactorily expressible, in some symbolic form or other. The feeling becomes matched with a formulation; it becomes known, and thus a useful part of personality structure.

Meltzer was the first, and is still the most complex, interpreter of Bion's overall picture of psychic growth. In *The Kleinian Development* (1978), in a detailed, penetrating and idiosyncratic analysis, inspired without being apostolic, he traces chronologically the evolution of Bion's theory of thinking from its group-researched roots (resulting in a distinction between mental and protomental), through learning from experience, container–contained and the chains of memory and desire, to the crucial role of emotional turbulence and catastrophic change at growth-points of the personality. In this he saw Bion as re-using certain central tenets of Freud, such as interposing thought between impulse and action. Bion's model of growth is founded on intuitive speculation about the mother–baby relationship as the origins of alpha-function (symbol formation) in maternal reverie, in which the mother processes intolerable emotions on behalf of the baby and returns them in a contained form with the sense of being understood. This is the prototype for future learning from experience at all phases of development, and constitutes the origins of thinking, which continues to be an object-related phenomenon.

The emotional dynamics oscillate between the paranoid-schizoid and the depressive positions, in a continuing spiral movement, expanding the existing structure of the personality. The emotional turbulence entailed causes 'suffering', Bion's term for anxiety which is being usefully processed rather than evacuated. At the moment of breakthrough to the depressive position (which he terms 'intersection with O'), attained through 'catastrophic change', there is a momentary sense of truth, harmony – an aesthetic feeling, which is almost immediately superseded by the next conflict on the horizon with its clouds of doubt and ambivalence. This ongoing process he terms 'thinking' or 'useful work'. This kind of 'work group', whether entirely internal or external (as in an intimate couple relationship), contrasts with the basic assumption mentality of the established group (again, internal or external) which resists change.

Meanwhile the enemy within is seen less in terms of narcissism, omnipotence or paranoia, but as primarily a liar or mind-poisoner which promotes 'alpha-function in reverse', in retreat from a half-glimpsed truth. Defences may now be seen as lies, deliberate obscurings. As an example he cites the dream of a patient of an old woman whose fingernails had been driven up her arm, 'so horribly deformed that no idea could be established of her previous state' ([1986] 2018), p. 134); this illustrates the attack on thinking, not simply of feeling as in a standard Kleinian formulation. Meltzer emphasised the formula LHK (love, hate, knowledge) and its antithesis, minus LHK – the Negative Grid which Bion indicated, though never fully developed. This picture of emotional links lies behind Meltzer's formulation of 'aesthetic conflict'. All in all it is an expansion of the Kleinian model rather than a replacement.

Evolutionary ethics (Money-Kyrle)

In addition to this revised theory of affects, the post-Kleinian model crucially expands on the role of internal objects which is fundamental to Klein's vision. It was not only Bion who was instrumental in this; indeed his abstract vision ('O') is harder to grasp than the more concrete one of Roger Money-Kyrle, also an analysand of Klein's and a trained philosopher. Meltzer was a great admirer of Money-Kyrle and worked closely with him for many years even before he began to study Bion in depth in the mid-1970s. All these thinkers see themselves as set firmly in the Platonic tradition with its concept of a realm of ultimate truth or reality, unknowable to mortal existence and infinite in extent, but nonetheless sensed in everyday life and the source of governing ethical principles. These principles are imperfectly known, always in flux, and may be followed or denied, supplanted. Platonism supports the view of mediated levels of knowledge, in which truth or reality filters down to the self, via internal objects, finding a symbolic form which is an aspect of truth, even though never the whole truth, but clothed or fictionalised in a digestible way.

Both Bion and Money-Kyrle point out that what is introjected during contact with internal objects is not just the thought or understanding of a conflict, but a function: the operation of the object, its capacity for thought. The self learns from the most advanced part of the mind not just an answer but a method: the container is internalised too (Money-Kyrle, 1968). This is a significant addition to the original Kleinian model. As Bion puts the same idea at the end of *Attention and Interpretation:*

> What is to be sought is an activity that is both the restoration of god (the Mother) and the evolution of god (the formless, infinite, ineffable, non-existent), which can be found only in the state in which there is *no* memory, desire, understanding.
> (Bion 1970, p. 129)

It is crucial that the realms of true knowledge are considered infinite – Plato's realm of Ideas. This progression gives direction to psychic development, which proceeds through mediation via the internal objects who are themselves evolving, but are always at a more advanced stage than the everyday or 'baby' self. Since everyone's internal objects, functioning like personal gods, are different and idiosyncratic according to their state of evolution, they cannot be classified and there can be no formulable goals; though inevitably there are vast areas of overlap between individuals.

After his chronological survey of Bion's theory in *The Kleinian Development* came *Studies in Extended Metapsychology* (1986) which was based largely on supervision material to which he applied the new Bionian perspective, and in whose 'Denouement' he also evaluated the significance of his own assimilation of Bion's ideas under the heading 'This is how it has come into my consulting room' ([1986] 2018), p. xvi). In the following sections, bearing in mind this underlying picture of the logical evolution of psychoanalysis, I shall look at Meltzer's own contribution to the post-Kleinian model, where again, the impact of Bion's ideas affirmed and expanded rather than essentially altering his own intrinsically 'aesthetic' viewpoint.

Key texts

Meltzer, D. ([1978] 2018). *The Kleinian Development*, 3 vols. London: Harris Meltzer Trust.

Meltzer, D. ([1986] 2018). *Studies in Extended Metapsychology*. London: Harris Meltzer Trust.

Chapter 2

Dream life and symbol formation

Meltzer saw psychoanalysis as 'a forcing house for symbol formation'; and by symbols, he meant autonomous symbols such as, primarily, dreams, in the context of their containment by the psychoanalytic setting and the transference–countertransference. 'The dream is my landscape', Meltzer wrote in a letter; and he describes dream-reading as his primary talent:

> I discovered that I was a good reader of dreams, which seems utterly trivial – except that they are marvellous and mysterious and alert you to the fact that the human mind is something about which we actually know nothing.
> ([2002a] 2021, vol. 2, p. 169)

Anyone reading his books will see that dreams are the source of all his theories, or at least of his conviction about any of them, as well as his functioning as a clinician. He would not continue to work with patients who refused to bring dreams (as distinct from having difficulty remembering them), believing that everyone dreams and that remembering them is a sure indication of the desire to cooperate in the analytic work. In dreams, autonomous symbols are created, rather than relying upon received (conventional) symbols which should properly be called 'signs' since they are pointers to an agreed meaning, rather than containers for a new meaning that has

DOI: 10.4324/9780367822828-4

only just found its place in the psyche – something which happens, potentially, in every psychoanalytic session.

Revising the Freudian theory

Meltzer thought Freud's theory of 'day residue' and 'decoding' was inadequate and his theory that the function of dreams was to keep the dreamer asleep was strangely offbeam – Meltzer says he could not possibly have believed; it followed from his neurophysiological model, rather than from his practice. Decoding assumes dream content can be verbally explained, substituted, like bad literary criticism. In Meltzer's view, dreams are mental events in which psychic relationships are not merely represented in metaphor but enacted and developed:

> There are dreams, as Emily Bronte said, which 'go through one's life like wine through water', enriching one's vision of the world with an intoxication of emotional colouring as never before … When such a dream has visited our sleeping soul, how can we ever again doubt that dreams are 'events' in our lives? In this dream world is determined the great option between an optimistic and a pessimistic view, not only of our own lives, but of Life.
>
> ([1984] 2018), p. 101)

Dreams, therefore, *have meaning* – as indeed, literature and tradition have always believed – and not only this, they can *create meaning* through symbols which radically change the personality and set it on a new path. Dream life, like art, is a 'presentational form', which needs not to be decoded but to be received, contained, matched to another mind. Meltzer said that Ella Freeman Sharpe, in her book *Dream Analysis,* was the only analyst of that era to have taken a 'quietly divergent' view from Freud's; as a literary person she observed and pointed out the 'poetic diction' of dreams with their musical and evocative rhetorical devices. Yet epistemological and metaphysical problems still remained in connection with their meaning and purpose. There was the question 'Can I know that I am dreaming?' and also 'Can I know what someone else has dreamed?' pointing to the difference between dreaming and remembering a dream, which is already a transformation in preparation for communication.

Meltzer, like Bion, often invoked Freud's special definition of consciousness as an 'organ for the perception of psychic qualities', with its emphasis on the internal quality of scientific observation, subsumed by Bion under the idea of 'attention'. As Bion said, the organ of consciousness can be directed inward (when asleep) or outward (when awake). Thus waking and consciousness are not the same:

> When is someone 'completely' asleep, or 'deeply' so, as compared to 'dozing' or 'half-asleep'? Had he taken greater heed of his own definition of consciousness as an 'organ for the perception of psychic qualities', he would have had very little difficulty in framing a directional definition in regard to this organ's orientation towards external and internal phenomena, even if he had not taken such a concrete view of psychic reality as Melanie Klein embraced.
>
> ([1984] 2018, p. 23)

The Kleinian view of spaces and of unconscious phantasy replaced that of primary process as a working model. The 'theatre of phantasy' is populated by objects and part-objects, a dramatic scenario which Meltzer said he saw daily in the consulting room. In later days he felt in fact that some analysts had lost touch with Melanie Klein's own stress on the psychic reality of the part-object figures of the inner world, their values and functions, and with the psychic space or spaces which they inhabit. It is the theatre of phantasy, where meaning is generated, that unites adult dreaming with children's play.

Just as Susan Isaacs (1948) drew out the implications of Klein's view of unconscious phantasy, Meltzer made explicit the idea of dream-life as continuous unconscious phantasy, of which the psychoanalyst is offered a 'privileged sampling': thus reorienting the psychoanalytic session to mental life as a whole, in both analyst and analysand. The recognition of a concrete inner world made it possible to distinguish symbol formation from concreteness of thought (as in Hanna Segal's [1957] 'symbolic equation') which is a psychotic phenomenon having to do with the person's feelings about how his thoughts have an impact on things and people in the outside world.

Dreams are observed, remembered, discovered, but not invented. Regardless of their quality, which varies over the entire spectrum from humdrum to poetic, they are free from the chains of omnipotent pseudo-thinking. Unlike any other type of association, dreams tell the truth about our emotional experiences even when their content is depicting the denial of emotional reality. The potential for dreams to actually work out emotional problems (thinking) by means of unconscious drama only made sense with support from Bion's emotion-based theory of knowledge. So dream-life is the most truthful representation of the actual transactions of objects within the inner world and thus of the mind's current conflicts and state of development.

By virtue of the mind's ability to observe itself, this includes dreams that tell the story of the various anti-thinking processes, so helping to think about them. 'Fragments of incipient thought' that are suspended in an 'uncertainty cloud' may either be gathered into a symbol, clarifying the confusion, or take refuge in somatic symptoms or in the non-thinking social organisation of basic assumption groupings.

An aesthetic theory of dreams

Meltzer was well read in the philosophy of symbol formation, in the tradition of Wittgenstein, Cassirer, Whitehead and Langer. This is the tradition that is particularly concerned with the distinction between 'discursive' and 'presentational' forms', saying and showing – the limitations of conscious meaning versus the richness of unconscious meaning. Language, as a symbolic mode, has two functions and two roots: one concerned with communication of information, the other concerned with communicating states of mind.

True symbols, as containers for ideas, are not just ways of communicating, but the means of mental growth; and their origin in the unconscious is bound up with the entire network of these object relations. It is most clearly understood in terms of the child learning language, which is reactivated each time an autonomous symbol is created in adulthood. Meltzer differentiates the information-theory philosophies of language (which equate word and idea) from the grammar of unconscious phantasy:

> In our theory, grammar would stand in an absolutely bound relation to the language of unconscious phantasy in something of the same relation as a scale of tones stands to a body of music; or as the particular set of axioms stands in relation to the body of a particular geometry; or as a particular set of 'natural rights' stands in relation to a body of law and what the courts will do in fact.
>
> ([1984] 2018, p. 119)

Grammar is a function of 'inner language' and of object relations, rooted in the child's instinctual capacity and wish to convey its emotional state – the 'song and dance' view of the origins of language. In the Cassirer tradition, this inner language is the source of all the symbolic forms (art, music, etc.). In terms of verbal language, the child moves from vocalisation to verbalisation, in which the inner language adapts to external reality and the agreed notational system of the culture. The skill of the poet consists in matching depth grammar (the emotional level) with surface grammar; and both levels are found in dreams, with their primarily visual but also verbal representations.

It was in the context of this philosophical tradition that, in *Dream Life* (1984), he said he was trying to 'formulate an aesthetic theory of dreams' (p. 29) that would bring psychoanalysis more in line with traditional art forms – both their methodology and their focus on dream-symbols. Intimate relations and art forms are parallel examples of the processing of dream life, and subsequent to Bion's work, all these intimate areas can be seen to contrast with the 'protomental' or adaptational forms of existence which represent the equivalent of language's lexical or surface grammar rather than its poetic 'deep' grammar. This includes all the features of musical diction, tone, resonance, dynamics, etc., which are lost in a standard written notation.

Vocalisation in dreams therefore stands in a 'fugue relation' to the visual nature of the dream as plastic symbolic form:

> In preferring to relate the two as 'fugue' rather than to speak of them as 'parallel' we would wish to imply a creative interaction by means of which the two symbolic forms potentiate one another in capturing meaning. This brings to a new poignancy Ella Sharpe's delineation of the 'poetic diction' of the dream process and builds a bridge to the field of aesthetics in general. It would seem to open up to investigation the area of 'composition' of the dream as an aesthetic object.
>
> ([1984] 2018, p. 123)

As with symbols in general, an interactive drama is taking place, not just a pointing to a codified meaning. Of the aesthetic containing power of certain dreams, Meltzer wrote:

> It can be seen that a number of central *formal* structures are being drawn up into juxtapositions to create a space scintillating with potentiated meaning. Sometimes words and visual forms are seen to interact … At other times spaces are being created

as containers of meaning. At other times the movements from one type of space to another, and the emotional difficulties of making such moves, are made apparent.

(p. 165)

Individual dreams – like all symbols – may vary greatly in their aesthetic quality: their formal organisation, and richness of metaphor. However they always contain infinitely more meaning than the patient, or the analyst, can verbalise. They represent the most creative level of an individual's mental functioning. Indeed, this is the only functioning that is truly mental; everything else is either protomental (in Bion's term) or discursive – that is, it 'says' rather than 'shows' things, and what can be 'said' is inevitably much less complex than what can be 'shown' in dreams or other symbolic modes such as art forms. Dream-life is the place in which mental growth occurs: 'growth goes on in the quiet chrysalis of dream-life' (p. 177). It occurs (or is stunted) whether or not we are privileged to observe it, and whether or not we can find a reasonably correct interpretation for the dream. In dreams, mental life *happens* and – as Keats would say – 'the creative creates itself'.

Symbol formation

Psychoanalysis has always been concerned with symbol formation but again, the definition has progressed from an equation between symbols and signs (fixed denominations) to that of autonomous symbols as containers for meaning, evolving within a particular emotional situation. 'A symbol is not a sign, it is a device for linking which expresses a congruence but implies an increment of meaning to both' (Meltzer & Williams [1988] 2018, p. 77). Melanie Klein thought the capacity for symbol formation was essential to the development of the child, as manifest in play; Hanna Segal in the early 1950s defined the nature of 'symbolic equations' where the symbol is taken to be same as the thing symbolised – that is, a pseudo-symbol which has not been processed through abstraction and 'reparation' (in effect, by internal objects, in the depressive position). Meltzer often refers to this core feature of the Kleinian development. It was he however who linked the Cassirer philosophical tradition (which indeed really began with Coleridge) with the psychoanalytic investigation of dreams, and who specifically linked symbol formation with Bion's 'learning from experience', as distinct from the sign-language of conventional grammar. He said that an important indicator of analytic progress was the quality of the patient's dreaming, generally moving from long anecdotal dreams to short condensed symbolic dreams.

In a paper on 'Symbol and allegory', Meltzer gives dream-examples from the same patient to illustrate the difference between creative and fixed symbol formation. The dreams are not only symbols in themselves, they are about symbol formation. The first, most complex dream concerned a landscape with 'three levels' in which 'nations were on the move': one level an arid African plain, another an arid plateau, each with people fleeing towards or away from persecution, and a rich grassland where people were also moving but in no hurry to either arrive or leave anywhere – they were not refugees bound by either the past or the future (memory or desire). Meltzer comments:

> This seems to me to be the essential structure of symbol formation – complex moving at many different levels ... On this verdant level it was possible for people to live in some sort of peace and to see the horizon in a way that informed them the earth was not flat, but that they were living on an object moving in space, in a system that had its own laws ... an awareness that we live as part of a planetary system.
>
> ([2000a] 2021, p. 129)

This psychological 'planetary system' he associates with 'the family which is the planetary unit of human life'; those children, or parts of the personality, that lose their centre of gravity fall into 'despair'.

By contrast, Meltzer then cites another dream from the same patient in which people were on a large pleasure cruising boat with a luxurious interior, and outside, there was a flower garden on the forward deck and a churchyard with tombstones at the stern. Meltzer saw this as an emblem of the traditional 'ship of fools', an allegorical rather than symbolic metaphor of birth, life and death: nine months in the comfort of the womb, followed by an 'evanescent blossoming and then head for the graveyard'. This ship is the product of human ingenuity, like a surrealistic painting (a genre Meltzer saw as pseudo-imaginative): an attitude which mocks the optimism that is open to unknown possibilities and mystery – the true way forward for humanity. The meaning is fixed, painted on by an omniscient codifier who appears very clever and yet (as Meltzer says elsewhere) this type of vision is not really so clever since they invented the code so of course they can undo it.

Meltzer considers that this cynical stance of knowing everything already – believing that everything is the product of human ingenuity – also illuminates the nature of thought disorder. In a paper on 'Thought disorder' he refers to three patients, all 'fun to work with' and 'gifted talkers', yet whose bark had little bite – little genuine substance:

> They are all gifted talkers with a vocabulary that bespeaks their basic intelligence but tends to make little or no sense. This gives the 'barking' impression even when not ostensibly attacking. They have a free flow of associations which are not always to the point but often tangential to the topic. The general impression is of strongly suppressed violence which takes the form of silent obscenities during or just after the session.
>
> (2005b, p. 423)

The 'bark' seems to represent 'an overly hasty transformation into language in which vague, ambiguous and equivocal usages are interwoven without discrimination'. There is a 'premature nomination' – that is, a name or categorisation replaces the description of an event. Or there is some other way to obscure the facts, some rationalisation. Thus one patient accused the analyst of marketing his own brand of 'shit cream', which did indeed make him analyse what he meant by 'thought disorder'; in that particular instance it was not evidenced by a dream but by a strangely illogical account of a minor car collision where the patient's calculation of the other car's speed was clearly totally absurd.

> The overall impression is of children who cannot understand why their plans do not work. The result is a simmering disappointment and dissatisfaction with the world which does not obey them, for they are born teachers and disciplinarians with a stick-and-carrot mentality. It is most difficult of all for them to feel puzzled rather than frustrated.
>
> (2005b, p. 424)

And the meaning of the manufactured evidence is supposed to be evident to anybody except the analyst, who is an idiot for not understanding.

Key text

Meltzer, D. ([1984] 2018). *Dream Life*. London: Harris Meltzer Trust.

Chapter 3

An expanded view of identification

The psychoanalytic view of the nature of identification processes has steadily expanded since Freud's original idea about 'primary identification' with the object (in the oral period) being superseded by the internalisation of the objects in the ego, following the resolution of the Oedipus complex. In Meltzer's history of the psychoanalytic model, it was Klein's resituating all conflicts in relation to the mother's body as a phantasy world that resulted in a proliferation in the possibilities of identification. The concept of narcissism was now seen not in terms of libido but in terms of the organisation of infantile parts of the self *vis-à-vis* internal object relations. This led also to a new understanding of transference as something happening in the present rather than archaeologically excavated and repeated from the past.

Projective identification

The revelation of the mother's body as a world with spaces and infinite sub-spaces, that could be entered into or imagined in phantasy life, lent itself to endless investigation in its illumination of psychopathology and the phenomena of the consulting room. The structural shift in the psychoanalytic model that resulted from Mrs Klein's work enabled a deeper investigation of projective identification by her followers; Meltzer notes Rosenfeld's work on

DOI: 10.4324/9780367822828-5

narcissistic organisations and on hypochondria with its projective and introjective aspects, and Segal's work on depression in the schizophrenic, demonstrating the ways in which mental pain can be distributed by projective identification into external objects.

Then finally, Bion transformed the concept of projective identification into an operation with a whole spectrum of meanings, ranging from pathological evacuation to primitive preverbal communication, the developmental basis of the mother–baby relationship; instead of talking about 'normal' *versus* 'excessive' degrees of projective identification,

> Bion ... attributed a specific and essential function in primitive communication between the mother and baby to this operation, thus also laying the basis for a new approach to understanding the nonlexical aspects of verbal communication in particular and non-verbal communication in general.
>
> ([1986] 2018, p. 48)

From as early as *The Psychoanalytical Process* (1967) Meltzer had written of 'intrusive' projection, suggesting that 'projective identification' was not the right term for Mrs Klein's original description of a pathological mechanism for entering and controlling another person. (And although she postulated this as a phantasy, Meltzer said she was well aware that it was not *only* a phantasy but could also affect the recipient.) In his paper 'Projective identification and container–contained' he clarifies that what is needed is a qualitative differentiation between communicative and tyrannical intentions:

Projective identification – the unconscious phantasy implementing the non-lexical aspects of language and behaviour, aimed at communication rather than action (Bion).
Intrusive identification – the unconscious omnipotent phantasy, mechanism of defence (Melanie Klein) ([1986] 2018, p. 71).

He then links the two poles of projective identification with the two types of 'container' that are being projected into, resulting in either a communicative link with a creative object or a destructive link with a pathological one:

Claustrum – the inside of the object penetrated by intrusive identification.
Container – the inside of the object receptive of projective identification (p. 71).

This expansion of the concept to include identification with the *inside* of the internal object, as delineated in his theory of the Claustrum, is perhaps Meltzer's most original contribution to the psychoanalytic model. It supersedes the 'quantitative' distinctions customarily made (such as 'excessive' or 'massive'). This new 'qualitative' framework for projective identification, separating the communicative from the intrusive, supported Meltzer's longstanding and increasing interest in the nature and origins of language and its relation to the psychoanalytic dialogue, with its foundation in the mother–baby prototype.

It will be seen that Meltzer bases his definition on widening the concept of projective identification to include 'the inside of the object'. By this he means primarily the inside of the *internal* object. This is one of his most significant modifications or expansions of the standard Kleinian model, though again, he would see it as implicit in the way Melanie Klein worked, owing to her focus on the psychic reality manifest in the transference through which the analyst represents the object, rather than on the external or environmental realities outside the consulting room. (More will be said below about intrusive penetration of the object and the variations of the Claustrum which result.)

Introjective identification

Within this expanded scheme of projective identification Meltzer rescues the concept of introjection from the earlier perception of its being a possessive psychic move to swallow the (idealised) object whole, whilst splitting off the unwanted parts through evacuative projection. Instead (as is probably assumed by most analysts these days), the true introjective movement is seen as part of an ebb-and-flow with the communicative-projective, as in Bion's reverie and alpha-function: the basis for imbibing knowledge. To this picture of the baby learning is added the reciprocal learning of the mother from the baby. Meltzer (unlike Bion) was immersed in infant observation, owing to working with Esther Bick, Martha Harris and their students, teaching in a variety of countries. He had a wealth of material to draw upon, hence can say:

> I think that introjective identification is something that comes about in a most mysterious way through an intensely cooperative relationship between an object that wishes to project and an object that wishes to accept the projection. It's not only the baby that introjects from the breast, it's also the mother who introjects the baby. Not simply accepts the projection of distressed parts of the self as Dr Bion has described in order to return them to the baby in a less distressed state. The mother does also introject the baby as a person in her internal world, and the baby introjects from the mother not simply a breast or nipple and not simply a mother, but introjects what the mother wishes to project into the baby which generally we assume is a mother and father, a united couple, a combined object.
> (From a talk in 1979, unpublished)

Introjection is thus a complex process which is enabled by projection, in the context of a two-way communicative link between mother and baby, or baby and adult parts of the personality. It is seen by both Bick and Harris as foundational to containing the infantile personality, and to identifying with parental integrative functions, not just the satisfaction of needs or wishes. Activating this latent parental function depends on an active reciprocity, a mutual learning from experience. As Bick puts it:

> The internal function of containing the parts of the self is dependent initially on the introjection of an external object,

experienced as capable of fulfilling this function ... The need for a containing object would seem, in the infantile unintegrated state, to produce a frantic search for an object – a light, a voice, a smell, or other sensual object – which can hold the attention and thereby be experienced, momentarily at least, as holding the parts of the personality together. The optimal object is the nipple in the mouth, together with the holding and talking and familiar smelling mother.

(Bick 1968 [2018], p. 140)

Infant observation teachers would point out that the baby 'knows' its need to develop, as well as desiring comfort or gratification; the baby seeks through reciprocity a source of understanding. And this, as Harris points out, depends upon 'introjective identification with valued internal parental figures' on the part of the mother or caregiver (Harris [1978] 2018), p. 39); self-knowledge takes place through mediated links.

One could say then that the thinking, working mind of the mother, which leads her to respond specifically and appropriately, is the basis for introjecting a benign combined object—a developing and not a static one.

(Harris [1982] 2018), p. 67)

Introjection, initiated in infancy, in association with communicative projective identification, then becomes the prototype for learning from experience throughout life. It is always experienced as 'a mind-to-mind process', not an omnipotent acquisition. Like the chaotic sense data bombarding the baby, every new idea is attended by turbulence and confusion, and arouses anxiety; it then requires ordering by either an external or internal object in the role of a parental transference. Meltzer summarises this post-Kleinian picture of personality development:

The learning consequent has therefore *the meaning of an item of introjective identification* since not only is the immediate problem resolved (secondary learning of knowledge or skill) but also something is learned of the modes of thought employed in the resolution (primary learning: Wittgenstein's 'now I can go on'). The dependent relation to the internal or external tutor requires a struggle from the paranoid-schizoid to a depressive orientation (Bion's Ps↔D) since the meaning and significance must be entertained as an aesthetic experience.

([1986] 2018, p. 179)

Mind-to-mind and container–contained

One of the implications of seeing this prototypal relationship as a mind-to-mind process is the logical conclusion that, in its analytic form, the analytic couple require containment by the process itself. It is not simply that the analyst contains the emotional conflicts of the analysand. As Meltzer puts it in his 'Denouement' to *Studies in Extended Metapsychology*:

> The model of container–contained places a new value on receptiveness and the holding of the dynamic situation of transference–countertransference in the mind. But perhaps to state this as if the analyst were the container misses the point that it is the fitting together of the analyst's attention and attitudes to the cooperativeness of the patient that forms and seals the container, lending it the degree of flexibility and resilience required from moment to moment.
>
> ([1986] 2018, pp. 149–250)

Meltzer spells out and draws together the implications of Bion's container–contained formulation with its stress on links rather than weighting one or other endpoint of a relationship. Container–contained he regards as a higher level of abstraction than projective identification, in terms of Bion's Grid ([1986] 2018, p. 49); but it is part of the same system by which a thinking process is set in motion. Learning from experience requires a link in which more than one party, vertex or facet of the mind is engaged in the process of changing and developing. Meltzer, more than Bion, is definite about his reliance on the analytic setting and its containment of the analytic process (more is said about this in Part II). It results from a model of the mind in which a mother–baby type partnership attempts to find symbols for an emotional experience, for which the relationship itself provides containment and support. The symbol containing the meaning is created not just within but *by* the relationship. The dynamics are the interweaving of projection and introjection, oscillating between paranoid-schizoid disquiet and depressive acceptance, in a continuing pattern that traverses the whole field of the transference.

Where the original Kleinian model would have emphasised the potential destructiveness caused by attacks on the good object from envy and paranoia, the expanded post-Kleinian model recognises the potential trauma caused by the developmental process itself. Bion describes how a new thought trying to enter the mind is experienced as violent and destructive; it is not welcomed as the way forward, but rather is an underlying source of anxiety. The personality would rather remain quiet and stable, retaining its existing shape and status; but of course it cannot do so without rigidifying, which results in psychic death. Meltzer says this is particularly evident when working with children:

> The later addition of 'catastrophic change' served to emphasise the violence of the forces of thought requiring containment, and the particular need for a container which was neither too rigid nor too flexible, so that the new idea could develop and yet not destroy its container by its expansive thrust. It will become clear in the clinical material how germane to the experience of children is the Bionic description or model.
> ([1986] 2018, p. 49)

(The clinical material referred to, by three child psychotherapists, concerns the many different ways in which the child seeks to symbolise the experience of union and separateness from the mother, depicted in relation to parts of her body; and the struggle between communicative modes and intrusive or triumphant modes, which result in a Claustrum rather than a container.)

Adhesive identification

The concept of adhesive identification was developed by Meltzer in association with Bick's observations on psychic skin. Adhesive identification is neither projective nor introjective; the Kleinian spatial model brings it to light, since the problem reveals itself through two-dimensionality. Meltzer worked very closely with Bick who, he said, revealed the identificatory processes connected with two-dimensionality that result in adhesive identification. Bick described how the first 'container' is experienced as a skin holding the body together, and how some infants come up with a 'second-skin' false container as a substitute for reliance on the real container when this is felt as inadequate. The phenomenon of adhesive identification seemed at first to indicate a phase in mental development earlier than the paranoid-schizoid position; though it then became apparent that it was not a matter of maturity but of a defence that Meltzer called 'dismantling' the senses in order to avoid aesthetic impact.

For several years in the early 1970s Meltzer worked with and supervised colleagues who were treating children diagnosed with early infantile autism, later documented in *Explorations in Autism* (1975) with John Bremner, Shirley Hoxter, Doreen Weddell and Isca Wittenberg. Autism was a newly recognised condition, more specific then than in the current use of the term which in practice encompasses a range of problems. In the book, its acknowledged narrowness and specificity enabled a focus on particular aspects of mental development and on how they could get stuck. It would become crucial to his understanding of the aesthetic nature of development and its reliance on 'aesthetic conflict'. This group of children embodied for Meltzer a single mentality: he saw them as representing particular phases of the condition, as if they were one child at various stages of emergence, and the book itself was a 'traveller's tale' through this mental terrain. For him the children acquired almost a certain heroism owing to their aesthetic sensibility and innate desire to avoid violence. He said that in working with them problems were located rather than solved:

> We believe we have located some very mysterious phenomena of the mind by recognising them operative in very condensed form in the children treated. These phenomena, of dismantling, impairment of spatial and temporal concepts, employment of mindlessness as a temporising move – all these seem to us to throw a very bright beam on modes of thought and relationship discernible elsewhere, in normal or ill people, in the analytic consulting room as in everyday life.
> ([1975] 2018, p. 3)

The concept of mindlessness opened a 'vast area' to scrutiny, not remotely understood. Nonetheless the location of these problems did expand the understanding of the existing spatial model of the mind, bringing into logical focus the significance of aesthetic experience as a universal developmental crux – something Meltzer had always suspected but which found no theoretical foundation. It was Bion's postulation of the instinctive retreat from emotionality, because developmental change is so alarming, that enabled this theoretical augmentation: Meltzer saw that retreat from emotionality meant retreat from aesthetic conflict. In the case of the autistic children, this retreat took the form of two-dimensionality. The qualities of the two-dimensional self he described as follows:

> Its experiences could not result in the introjection of objects or introjective modification of its existing objects. It could not therefore conduct in thought experiments in regression or progression from which the memory of past events could be reconstructed more or less accurately, and future possibilities

adumbrated with some degree of conviction. Its relationship to time would be essentially circular, since it would be unable to conceive of enduring change, and therefore of development – or cessation. Circumstances which threaten this changelessness would tend to be experienced as break-down of the surfaces – cracking, tearing, suppuration, dissolution, lichenification or ichthyotic desensitising, freezing numbness, or a diffuse, meaningless, and therefore tormenting sensation such as itching.

(pp. 227–228)

A logical cognitive and emotional step was missing in these children, between two-and three-dimensionality: namely, the capacity for splitting and idealisation which Klein had put forward as the foundation stone of healthy development, and which Meltzer points out is 'the necessary pre-condition to the container function' (p. 237). In Bion's terms they had no means of distinguishing between an 'absent (good) object' and a persecuting absent object (so means of establishing a container). Meltzer suggested that the reason for this was 'the lack of an internal space within the mind in which phantasy as trial action, and therefore experimental thought, could take place' (p. 227). Instead of existing in three dimensions, both self and object were conceived as two-dimensional surfaces:

> Where Mrs Bick has demonstrated a step in mental organisation of experience proximal in time to the operation of splitting-and-idealisation (which in its turn is preconditional to splittingand-projective-identification), we are attempting a further step. Instead of defects in the container-function of the object we are attempting to describe defects in the conception-ofthe-object-as-a-container, namely the two-dimensional conception.
>
> (p. 237)

Although these surfaces were experienced with great sensitivity, such a conception of the world (both inner and outer) was non-developmental as the dialogue between projection and introjection was not possible. The children glued their own surface to that of the object, in order to avoid destructive attacks – separation was simply negated:

> While the child in projective identification will experience the refusal of his tyranny as a threat to his omnipotence and reduplicate his efforts, a similar refusal in the case of adhesive identification produces collapse, as if torn off and thrown away by the object.
>
> (p. 231)

Indeed the way out of the autistic condition entailed getting in touch with their own aggression and destructiveness, acquiring the ability to split good from bad, thus opening up dimensionality.

Related to two-dimensionality was the tendency of the more ill children to 'dismantle their senses', that is, to keep the information from their senses separate. This was the opposite of the 'consensuality' Meltzer cites from Harry Stack Sullivan, similar to Bion's 'common sense' and necessary to the symbol formation that gives meaning to the world. This consensual knowledge was warded off by what he terms 'exquisitely delicate' means of diffusion of attention.

Meanwhile the adhesively identified child might often be supposed to be empty-headed, owing to their identification processes applying solely to the surface of objects; and their intelligence underestimated, just as the child (or adult) in fixed projective identification is liable to have their intelligence overestimated owing to mimicry of knowledge content. In Meltzer's picture it has nothing to do with intelligence, but rather with the nature of protomentality, as in Bion's denomination: a state prior to the real commencement of mental life. Adhesive identification means there is no containing object; projective identification means the container is under illusory or omnipotent control. But at least, in the latter case, the developmental drama has begun – the 'interplay between mental and protomental' that 'competes for the soul of the child' ([1986] 2018), p. xiii); and indeed, for the adult thereafter.

For protomentality – states that lie outside mental functioning proper – has many manifestations, including (Meltzer suggests) somatic ones, and most commonly, the automatic obedience to basic assumption groupings that Bion has described and that comprise a large part of our everyday life, both internal and external. It begins at the beginning of human relationships, as evidenced in work with children: there is an account of how 'A three-year-old uses the gang as container' (a seminar together with Martha Harris, recounted in Negri and Harris [2007]), and in another joint supervision with Harris, an account of a one-year-old coping with his new nursery environment by becoming a kind of bureaucrat, stamping each apple in the crate with a toothmark ('A one-year-old goes to nursery' in *Studies in Extended Metapsychology*).

In his review of the autism work in *Studies in Extended Metapsychology,* Meltzer looks back and analyses the crucial interconnection between all these factors, and their relevance to the extended Kleinian model of the mind. In particular he focused on the puzzling problem of the children's aesthetic sensibility yet their difficulties with symbol formation. What model of the mind could resolve, make sense of, this apparent contradiction?

> The fine aesthetic sensibility of many of these children was so unmistakable that one could not avoid wondering if their developmental failure had not been founded on processes for warding off the impact of the beauty of the world.
> ([1986] 2018, p. 245)

The two-dimensionality could now be seen as a method of toning down emotional intensity, and this was what resulted in the impoverished or diluted meaningfulness of their world.

It was in itself 'a defence against the impact of objects stirring emotions' – aesthetic objects.

But how? Melanie Klein's idea had been that interest in the inside of the mother, and thereby the epistemophilic instinct in general, had its origins in the intense emotionality of the mother–baby relationship. Did two-dimensionality then result from a denial of the psychic reality of the object rather than a regression to a prior stage in cognitive development?

(p. 245)

Instead of a regression to a more primitive stage, as he had first assumed, the autistic children were in fact employing a more sophisticated means of dissipating a meaning whose aesthetic impact they found intolerable, and to which they were particularly sensitive. Where the love and hate evoked were too intense, it was easier to remove the otherness of the object altogether by glueing to its surface, than to pursue the ambivalent implications of otherness and strive for knowledge and understanding.

This accounted for the impoverished capacity for symbol formation, which requires a three-dimensional relationship with the object, a recognition of other spaces outside the self. This is the precondition for the mental 'level' to be 'called into play', which Meltzer says only became clear as a result of Bion's protomental distinction that could indeed postulate the mind as operating on different levels simultaneously:

And so they came together: the key of alpha-function and the lock of two-dimensionality; and an apposite metaphor it seemed. The problem area that the key of symbol formation was called into play to open, was the enigma of the inside and the outside of the aesthetic object. Its power to evoke emotionality was only equalled by its ability to generate anxiety, doubt, distrust. While the sensual qualities of the aesthetic object could be apprehended with some degree of confidence, its internal qualities, being infra- or supra-sensual, carried no such comfort.

(p. 248)

Thus the experience with autistic children, which had features that seemed to fall outside the existing Kleinian model of the mother-space and the search for knowledge of it, was illuminated by adding in the Bionic idea of reaction against the emotional turbulence stirred by contact with reality. It seemed there were ingenious ways of escaping these ubiquitous human conflicts without actually enlisting on the devil's side.

Key texts

Meltzer, D. ([1975] 2018). *Explorations in Autism.* London: Harris Meltzer Trust.

Meltzer, D. ([1986] 2018). *Studies in Extended Metapsychology.* London: Harris Meltzer Trust.

Chapter 4

Aesthetic conflict

Clinical experience and supervision, with his view of the psychoanalytic process as an aesthetic experience in itself, were superimposed on Meltzer's longstanding interest in aesthetics and dovetailed into his formulation of aesthetic conflict as the key to developmental process. In *The Apprehension of Beauty* (1988) he attributes to Bion the pioneering conceptual speculation which made this synthesis possible:

> If we follow Bion's thought closely we see that the new idea presents itself as an 'emotional experience' of the beauty of the world and its wondrous organisation, descriptively closer to the noumenon, to Hamlet's 'heart of mystery'.
> (Meltzer & Williams [1988] 2018, p. 20)

Meltzer consistently sees himself as trying to give clinical substance to Bion's thought, and he seizes on the support it provides for his own aesthetic perspective:

> It was the experience over the years of seeing the evolution of personality structure in arrested development of autistic children such as Marja Schulman's James, Doreen Weddell's Barry (*Explorations in Autism*) or Diomira Petrelli's Francesco (*Studies in Extended Metapsychology*) that hardened to

DOI: 10.4324/9780367822828-6

conviction the long-held suspicion that aesthetic considerations played an important role in development.

(p. xxiv)

Aesthetic conflict is the tension between 'the aesthetic impact of the outside of the "beautiful" mother, available to the senses, and the enigmatic inside which must be construed by creative imagination' (p. 22). The child's question, at first sight of his therapist, 'Are you a woman or a flower?', evoked a glimpse of the reaction of the newborn to the first sight of its mother and of her breast. Another child born prematurely, with brain damage, was not developing as her mother (before the therapist's intervention) continued to see her as an 'ugly little clown' and could not see the beauty of her developmental potential: 'She never gave the impression of seeing the spark of internal beauty in this child ... she was a mother with a hole in her where a beautiful baby had been' (p. 55). The therapy helped to restore this aesthetic link between mother and child, the therapist adding to the mother's qualities in order to strengthen the child's inner world. Such 'daily beauty' (Shakespeare's phrase, cited by Meltzer) has internal and external aspects, each promoting a therapeutic effect.

In the wake of clinical cases such as these, the formulation of the aesthetic conflict was a logical move:

> The formulation of the aesthetic conflict followed easily and almost immediately opened a new way of approaching developmental conflicts, for it placed the turmoil over the present object in a fugue relation to those already extensively studied about the absent object. In between these two areas of conflict it was then possible to insert Bion's vision of 'the absent object as a present persecutor', that is, the space where the object used to be as a ghost of its former existence.
>
> (p. xxiv)

The crucial developmental crux originated in the turbulence of conflicting emotions aroused by the beauty of the mother (object) from the earliest moments after birth, setting a pattern to be repeated throughout life at growth-points of turbulence or catastrophic change (in Bion's formulation). It involved a rethink of the role of the present and absent object. In Meltzer's view it was the ambivalence aroused by the present object that was of greatest importance; the relation to the absent object followed in a secondary position. It is the present object with the unknowable inside that stimulates turbulence and the temptation to retreat into paranoid-schizoid mode. Meltzer said, 'This question, *is it beautiful inside?* is the essence of the depressive position'. The tension between the sensuous outside and the invisible inside arouses different types of curiosity and different ways of knowing: from intrusive and controlling (paranoid-schizoid) to imaginative (depressive).

Interest

This meant that the psychoanalytic model needed to change its view of the fundamental developmental struggle: instead of life and death instincts, the individual is torn 'between aesthetic sensibilities and the forces of philistinism, puritanism, cynicism and perversity', Bion's positive *versus* negative links. For Meltzer, this lifelong struggle is dynamised by 'interest'. Interest, rather than pleasure, marks the beginning of an aesthetic experience. It is aroused by an apprehension of aesthetic impact – something which philosophers such as Susanne Langer regard as the origins of human mentality, which is characterised by the tendency to form symbols of its experience: 'In the beginning was the aesthetic object, and the aesthetic object was the breast and the breast was the world' ([1986] 2018, p. 245). Meltzer follows Winnicott's description of the 'ordinary devoted mother', as the normal, usual, natural, regular state of things – but adds the word 'beautiful' as part of that ordinary, everyday relationship:

> He was right to use that word 'ordinary', with its overtones of regularity and custom, rather than the statistical 'average'. The

aesthetic experience of the mother with her baby is ordinary, regular, customary, for it has millennia behind it, sinceman first saw the world 'as' beautiful.

(Meltzer & Williams [1988] 2018, p. 17)

While the mother-and-baby couple provide an aesthetic and interesting experience for the outside observer, within the couple, aesthetic reciprocity links the partners in the form of mutual interest, not just love. Interest activates the epistemophilic instinct of the baby in an emotional drama, evoking love, hate and the desire to know the object and therefore the meaning of the relationship. In a key passage in *The Apprehension of Beauty* Meltzer imagines the baby's perspective on this extraordinary ordinariness:

> The ordinary beautiful devoted mother presents to her ordinary beautiful baby a complex object of overwhelming interest, both sensual and infrasensual. Her outward beauty, concentrated as it must be in her breast and her face, complicated in each case by her nipples and her eyes, bombards him with an emotional experience of a passionate quality, the result of his being able to see these objects as 'beautiful'. But the meaning of his mother's behaviour, of the appearance and disappearance of the breast and of the light in her eyes, of a face over which emotions pass like the shadows of clouds over the landscape, are unknown to him. He has, after all, come into a strange country where he knows neither the language nor the customary non-verbal cues and communications. The mother is enigmatic to him; she wears the Gioconda smile most of the time, and the music of her voice keeps shifting from major to minor key. Like 'K' (Kafka's, not Bion's), he must wait for decisions from the 'castle' of his mother's inner world. He is naturally on guard against unbridled optimism and trust, for has he not already had one dubious experience at her hands, from which he either escaped or was expelled – or perhaps he,

rather than his mother, was 'delivered' from the danger! Even at the moments of most satisfactory communication, nipple in mouth, she gives an ambiguous message, for although she takes the gnawing away from inside she gives a bursting thing which he must expel himself. Truly she giveth and she taketh away, both of good and bad things.

(Meltzer & Williams [1988] 2018, p. 22)

Thus the understanding of the overpowering impact of aesthetic experience makes a meaningful extension to the old concept of ambivalence. From the doubts of the baby (Kafka's K) about the intentions of the enigmatic beautiful mother arises a passionate interplay of love and hate in which both ends of the emotional spectrum are constructively engaged and from which springs the desire for knowledge (Bion's K). Hence the origins of symbol formation. By 'passion', Meltzer explains that he does not refer to intensity of emotion but to the dramatic interchange of emotionality – the 'links', as Bion terms them. Every emotion is valid and has a part to play; it is the absence of emotionality that is the killer. In the post-Kleinian model, instead of love versus hate, gratitude versus envy, there are positive links (LHK: love, hate, knowledge) which constitute a developmental field, and negative links (minus LHK) which are anti-developmental and anti-passionate. Tolerance of the emotional vibrations of passion (aesthetic conflict) gradually builds up into ego strength and resilience, resulting in the 'negative capability' – the tolerance of not-knowing – that for Keats defined a 'man of achievement' (p. 20) and that lies at the heart of learning from experience.

> For in the interplay of joy and pain, engendering the love (L) and hate (H) links of ambivalence, it is the quest for understanding (K-link) that rescues the relationship from impasse. This is the point at which negative capability exerts itself, where beauty and truth meet.
>
> (p. 28)

For the baby–mother model underlies all self-knowledge, as distinct from the accumulation of information (knowing about). It is reactivated in the form of internal dialogue whenever a new idea is on the horizon that has the potential to bring structural change to the existing personality. It is not of course the literal mother–baby relationship as it was for the patient in their life history; it is the internal mother–baby relationship that exists, ever-changing, and operative in the present moment. Otherwise everyone would be tied to a past that they can do nothing about, and future ideas would be closed off. But the observation of actual mothers and babies enables us to see better how the internal mother–baby functions in opening our minds to new ideas and new aspects of the world of reality.

The prenatal aesthetic

Moreover, as Bion's speculative concepts about the object relations involved in thinking began to be borne out through clinical and observational experience (primarily through Meltzer's supervision work), so it was suggested that the passionate LHK conjunction may have a prototype in prenatal experience. As indicated in the long passage above, Meltzer extends his imaginative ruminations on the baby's first aesthetic experience backwards beyond birth into prenatal life. He said that he had never encountered a patient however ill who had not been touched by this initial impact, the 'dazzle of the sunrise':

> If, in fact, for the ordinary beautiful baby with his ordinary devoted beautiful mother, this aesthetic impact is what greets his emergence into the world outside the womb, then the aesthetic conflict and the depressive position would be primary for development, and the paranoid-schizoid secondary – the consequence of his closing down his perceptual apertures against the dazzle of the sunrise. In Plato's terms he would hasten back into the cave.
>
> (p. 28)

As in a passage that he wrote for a book on babies by the Psychoanalytic Group of Barcelona, this sunrise is really the sense of an 'extraneous intelligence', and is contemporaneous with a spontaneous feeling of surprise (Shakespeare's 'brave new world'):

> This is an attempt to formulate a metapsychology of the neonate: its aloneness between feeds, ignorance of the mother's mentality, schooled only by the rhythm of her services, unable to form symbols and have meaningful dreams, bound to sensation, at best anecdotal in recollection, not even linear, on the verge of chaos. It is not surprising if it comes out sounding like Genesis. In the beginning was the feed. What we are relying on is the galvanising of intelligence by attention to the polarity, for it is not in the beginning was the formless infinite, but the placenta as the primary feeding object. We might call this the experience of *surprise* and rewrite our genesis as a process starting with birth and panic relieved by surprise, not only surprise at finding the breast but surprise at an extraneous intelligence, the beginning of revealed religion. All the functions described are the fruits of identification with the extraneous intelligence. In the beginning object relations and identification are simultaneous.
>
> (in Williams [2010] 2018, p. 136)

It was this perception of the primacy of aesthetic experience that led him to reverse the traditional Kleinian chronology of the paranoid-schizoid and depressive positions. At the same time, we can see how it also implies the pre-existence or readiness of the infant to experience aesthetic impact, even in the womb – the Platonic viewpoint to which Meltzer regularly refers, seeing the post-Kleinian model as in close alignment. Like Bion, and following Freud, he regards birth not as the beginning of life but as a 'caesura' which is both a separation and a continuation of the developing personality beyond its original embryonic medium. He writes:

> Proto-aesthetic experiences can well be imagined to have commenced in utero: 'rocked in the cradle of the deep' of his mother's graceful walk; lulled by the music of her voice set against the syncopation of his own heart-beat and hers; responding in dance like a little seal, playful as a puppy. But moments of anxiety, short of foetal distress, may also attack the foetus; maternal anxiety may also transmit itself through heartbeat, rigidity, trembling, jarring movements; perhaps a coital activity may be disturbing rather than enjoyable, perhaps again dependent on the quality of maternal emotion; maternal fatigue may transmit itself by loss of postural tone and graceless movement. Perhaps above all the foetus may feel his growth as the narrowing of his home in typical claustrophobic fashion and deduce that life exists beyond its familiar bounds, a shocking idea to a natural flat-earther. Imagination is a foraging impulse; it will find food for thought in the desert.
> (Meltzer & Williams [1988] 2018, p. 17)

In the essay 'On aesthetic reciprocity' Meltzer offers a longer and more detailed phantasy about mental origins in prenatal life and the preparation of the foetus for what Bion calls 'catastrophic change' – the first of many, and the basis of subsequent development. For the caesura of birth is simply the most graphic and dramatic of the changes that happen whenever a new idea is introjected. At the same time, relating to the preverbal realm, it is the least easily symbolised; and for that reason it is perhaps worth citing the whole passage here, as an example of the kind of idiosyncratic imagination that also finds a parallel in the consulting room, which requires the evolution of a private 'language of achievement' (Bion's phrase from Keats). In the voice of the foetus, beginning with the awareness of 'interest', Meltzer writes:

Aesthetic conflict 53

I have always found my world basically congenial ever since I began to find it interesting. When I was a fish I just swam about and had no thoughts, but once I found my friend Placenta we explored and shared our findings, I with humming and dancing, he with his reassuring souffle. It became clear that there were others on the other side who hummed a lot. One I could hear particularly well, a wonderful hummer. We thought of finding the Northwest Passage but it was too good a world to leave until it began to shrink. In fact it became quite unpleasantly restrictive, positively cramping, and when I pushed the walls they began to push back. I got cross and really kicked out, but this seemed to have an adverse effect, quite frightening squeezings. We decided to leave, though we both suspected we were being forced to emigrate to make room for some newcomer. I felt pretty angry at this usurpation, for I had lived there since the beginning of time, after all. So, foolishly, you might say, I kicked out with the full power of my immensely strong legs. Well, I must have done some damage for a proper earthquake ensued, a great chasm opened up revealing the Northwest Passage I'd dreamed about. I was rammed into it, head first, Placenta following, but somehow in the chaos of the next few minutes or years, we became separated. I never saw him again. At the end of the passage everything was different, surprising, marvellous – and terrifying. My body became suddenly dense and heavy, immovable; some delicious smelling stuff ran into my chest and I heard myself, not humming but screaming. They must have thought I was screaming at them, those huge and beautiful creatures, so strong they could lift me with one hand while I couldn't even lift my own head. But it was the beauty of one that overpowered me, and I could see from the way she looked at me that I was tiny and ugly and comic. Then I realised I was to be thrown away, for kicking and screaming, I suppose, or for being little and ugly, perhaps. But I felt that these few moments before the end were somehow precious, just looking at her, though it hurt my eyes and I had to shut them. And her humming, pure music! By this time I was beginning to dry up, shrivel, shiver with cold and be tormented by a gnawing inside I 'd never had while Placenta was with me. Then she showed me the most beautiful thing in the world, to blind me, I supposed so that I should not see the abyss. Quite kind, really. My mouth stopped screaming and started sucking the anaesthetic stuff with which I was to be 'put to sleep'. Very humane. I could die laughing and crying and dreaming of being huge and beloved of her.

(Meltzer & Williams [1988] 2018, pp. 44–45)

Meltzer calls his phantasy a 'silly tale with a grain of truth' – but 'evocative'. It is an example of what Bion recommends as 'giving your imagination an airing' – an exercise in allowing oneself to be open to the reception of an idea.

But as a phantasy – a form of artistic internal observation – it also has roots in scientific observation. In particular during the late 1970s and early 80s, Meltzer was supervising neuropsychiatric work by Romana Negri with premature infants, in the course of which it became clear (as reported in the example in *The Apprehension of Beauty*) that an aura of aesthetic reciprocity amongst the caregivers, in relation to the damaged infant, had a perceivable therapeutic effect, at a time when psyche and soma were still closely intertwined as they had been in utero. It is not enough to alleviate physical suffering; even at this stage there is also mental suffering. The work is recounted in Negri's book *The Newborn in the Intensive Care Unit.* As he typically does, Meltzer (in his foreword to the book) poses the new question within a historical perspective, beginning with Freud's observation that in the first instance the ego is a body-ego:

In the early days of psychoanalysis it seemed completely reasonable to ask such questions as: 'When is the neural apparatus

> sufficiently developed to enable it to perform certain functions?' This no longer seems a reasonable question, for it has hidden in it a subtext: 'When does the tiny animal become a human being?' ... There is no purpose to be served in asking, 'At what point in gestation do experiences – human experiences – begin?' They began many thousands of years ago with the beginnings of symbol-formation and the capacity to wonder, to question.
>
> ([1994] 2018, p. xix)

The baby 'knows' its mother from its gestation in the womb 'in a deeper and more complex sense than it will ever again "know" another being' – that is, the human capacity for the intimate knowing that enables learning from experience begins here. From the 'near-infinite' capacity of the brain for recall (a computer-like function) emerges a different capacity, that of creative memory (a mental function) – something that, he says, is demonstrated continually within a psychoanalysis, where unconscious observation emerges in dreams and other features of the transference, becoming available for symbol-formation.

> There is no need to ask when this process commences: it is in the tissues that the primary events take place, and in the building of structure – of the body and of the mind – that they are incarnate. Structure is memory. Thus it is that man's picture of his world and his story of his personal past is in constant re-construction and modification.
>
> ([1994] 2018, pp. xix–xx)

Meltzer, as always, anchors this philosophical picture in the 'phenomenology of the analytic consulting room, contained in the history of scientist-artists from Freud to Bion'. This model of the origins of human mentality is not purely abstract speculation but partly derives from, and is partly corroborated by, the phenomena of the transference, whose rich implications continue to be clarified by the increasing body of psychoanalytic work. This includes the potential of being able to observe children who have (psychically) failed to get born, resulting in hyperactivity or failure of symbol formation.

Key text

Meltzer, D., & Williams, M. H. ([1988] 2018). *The Apprehension of Beauty*. London: Harris Meltzer Trust.

Chapter 5
The Claustrum

Meltzer's view of the primacy of aesthetic response, and of this being bound up with the baby's relation to the mother's internal spaces as well as her external appearance, is the basis for his formulation of the 'Claustrum', the self-imprisonment resulting from all the various defences against aesthetic impact. He said he was happy to find a way of relinquishing the concept of the death instinct, which is in effect superseded by the picture of the Claustrum. Only the adhesive identification of autism differs from the psychic imprisonment caused by intrusive types of identification – and that because the spatial qualities of the object are in themselves denied, so intrusive control is not even a possibility. Meltzer writes:

> Formulation of the aesthetic conflict as an inside–outside problem, as a conflict between what could be perceived and what could only be construed, led directly to the problem of violence as violation: violation of the privacy of internal spaces and their representations. The integrating force of this view of violence made itself felt over the whole range of violations, physical and mental, of individual against individual, groups against individuals and group against group. The previously formulated distinction between group and gang (*Sexual States of Mind* and *Studies in Extended Metapsychology*) was given a new sharpness of import with respect to internal as well as to

external organisation, especially regarding sexual crimes and sexual perversions.

(Meltzer & Williams [1988] 2018, p. xxiv)

In sexuality as in other core areas, health or personal development is to be seen in terms of the creative privacy of the internal combined object, and pathology in terms of tyranny over the object by infantile or narcissistic internal organisations.

The concept of aesthetic conflict enables an expanded view of the omnipotent phantasy first described by Klein in her 1946 paper on schizoid mechanisms. It may now be seen as a retreat from the aesthetic conflict, a new orientation on almost all types of pathology. Meltzer in his summaries of psychoanalytic history observes that projective identification proved fertile ground for Klein's followers, who traced a wide range of pathological phenomena to this mechanism: including claustrophobia, agoraphobia, hypochondria, manic-depressive states, disturbances of thought and judgement and certain psychotic confusional states. Thus Herbert Rosenfeld clarified the nature of hypochondria in terms of projective identification with a suffering internal object; Hanna Segal demonstrated the ways in which mental pain can be distributed through projective identification into eternal objects. Where Klein's original theory was formulated in relation to intrusion into an external object, and was conceived as a phantasy, it later become apparent that this phantasy actually affected the mental state of the person being projected into, and moreover, that it operated with internal objects as well as external ones.

As a destructive phantasy this type of intrusive projective identification, when 'excessive', was seen to have a connection with certain types of masturbation and to result in disturbances known as pseudo-maturity or 'false self', since the narcissistic identification resulted in a corresponding alienation from one's true identity. Meltzer's contribution to this Kleinian expansion of types of projective identification began with a famous paper on anal masturbation and the 'delusion of clarity of insight' (1965; reprinted in *The Claustrum,* 1992); he joked that he was considered to be the inventor of anal masturbation. This became the basis for his comprehensive account of the various chambers of the Claustrum, which are referred to throughout his work in response to specific material, but only comprehensively organised in his book of that name. This could be done after his definitive presentation of the theory of aesthetic conflict, which gave the violated spaces of the Claustrum a clear rationale, and indeed, gave the nature of violence a new meaning.

Just as, after Bion, the paranoid-schizoid and depressive positions may be seen to be in a continuous oscillation which is therefore 'normal' or constructive, so Meltzer believes that dipping in and out of the Claustrum is likewise ubiquitous, and a necessary part of self-knowledge. It is the degree of fixedness that induces an actual psychosis. The Claustrum is the world of the negative – in the Bionic sense of the antithesis to thinking and emotional experience, and the perverse areas are 'anti-emotions' rather than hostile or destructive emotions requiring to be integrated; hence, as he explains in the 'Denouement' to *Studies in Extended Metapsychology,* 'when the perverse trends are recognised as anti-emotions, minus L, H and K [love, hate and knowledge], no ground need be yielded to them in compromise' ([1986] 2018, p. 252).

The perverse area is exposed as purely destructive, not as split-off vitality that needs to be integrated. Meltzer believed that all groups resemble a Claustrum compartment and tend towards basic assumption organisation – to unthinking conformity, obedience and hierarchy. Not only severely disturbed people, or those who appear well adapted but are actually severely disturbed underneath, but also neurotic and 'normal' people move in and out of the Claustrum all the time, just as we move in and out of the various basic assumption groupings with their political requirements of tyranny and submission.

By contrast, true ethics, which are 'limitless in evolution', emanate from an individual's internal objects and therefore cannot be standardised. Hence the need to be alert to the matter of which part of the self is in control of the organ of attention – consciousness – as this is what allows for flexibility of movement and can redirect the vertex of vision to the outside of the object. The hidden Claustrum may not even be felt as constrictive owing to our compulsive rushing around; to defend against the impact of beauty, we compartmentalise our life processes. Meltzer deduces that everyone has, somewhere, an infantile part of themselves dwelling within an internal object. However 'bright their object', it is unlikely to be 'unblemished' by an aspect or area in which their capacity for passionate experience is stifled – from which the complementary love and hate are excluded and so therefore is true knowing. For in Eliot's well-known phrase, 'mankind cannot bear very much reality'.

The three chambers of the Claustrum

The investigation of claustrophobic phenomena enabled a new, or expanded, vision of the concreteness of the inner world and its objects. The narrative that began to take shape in the paper on anal masturbation continued with further clinical discovery of the mind's internal geography, based primarily on dreams and on the 'concrete' evidence from analytic work with children (his own patients or others') during what he termed 'the richest period in my analytic life'. This resulted in redefining 'massive' projective identification in terms of claustrophobic phenomena, at the heart of sadomasochism and despair. It is not the amount or degree but the type of projection that is relevant – a qualitative definition.

The Meltzerian view of claustrophobic phenomena, that is, of psychic self-imprisonment, is characterised by his geographic-theological view of the psychoanalytic model of the mind established by Klein, and this differentiates it from most theories of psychic imprisonment or retreat, which are generally not founded on this absolute rootedness in the idea of a concrete inner world. For Meltzer, the Claustrum is not a metaphor but a description of psychic reality, founded on the infant's original innate preconception of the mother-as-the-world. Psychic reality is primary; it establishes the type of vision by which external reality becomes known and is interacted with. Internal objects evoke emotions; external objects have emotions deployed on to them. The mother is naturally compartmentalised by the 'baby' and each compartment may in phantasy be viewed from an outside or an inside position. The viewpoint from inside is what constitutes the Claustrum. It is by definition a distorted reality, since it relies upon an intrusive type of projective identification, looking from the inside out, from a position of illusory control, in the manner of a glove-puppet. For 'what more complete denial of psychic reality can there be than to be living inside it' – whether this relates to external (institutionalised) or internal basic assumption groupings:

> By contrasting the two views – that constructed by imagination and that 'discovered' by intrusion – we can also gain a meaningful differential of views-of-the-world as they are determined by psychic reality, in health and in disturbance.
>
> ([1992] 2018, p. 61)

Meltzer posits three main types of intrusive projection into the body of the internal mother: the rectum, genital and head/breast. The dominant type of intrusive identification determines whether the cubicle is experienced as 'a torture chamber, a hothouse of eroticism, or place of heavenly peace and rest' ([1992] 2018, p. 97). His picture of these compartments had been forming over many years and was first indicated in *Sexual States of Mind* in relation to the various orifices of the body and the distinction between adult and infantile sexuality.

To go from the top down, as he does in *The Claustrum*, life inside the head/breast is characterised by 'the delusion of clarity of insight', a type of false omniscience which is essentially an escape from the emotional responsibilities and humility of the outside view:

> Construed from outside, the mother's head/breast is seen as an object, partial or later integrated with other aspects of the whole mother, eventually as a combined object, nipple/eyes and breast/head, whose primary quality is richness. This richness, at first concrete and related to urgent need for nourishment, becomes diversified in its nuances: generosity, receptiveness, aesthetic reciprocity; understanding and all possible knowledge; the locus of symbol formation, and thus of art, poetry, imagination. Seen from the inside, influenced by the motives for the intrusion, the story is a very different one. Generosity becomes quid pro quo, receptiveness becomes inveiglement, reciprocity becomes collusion, understanding becomes penetration of secrets, knowledge becomes information, symbol formation becomes metonymy, art becomes fashion. Seen from outside, the mother's head/breast is industrious, burdened with responsibilities, prudent from foresight. Viewed from inside it is indolent, carefree, living only in the power of its momentary beauty and wealth.
>
> ([1992] 2018, p. 71)

The useful and ethical qualities that could be stimulated if the view from outside were maintained are instead perverted into a degraded substitute: from this stance of 'identificatory grandiosity' derives 'the self-styled genius, the critic, the connoisseur, the aesthete, the professional beauty, the rich man, the know-itall, the scramblers after fame and the "bubble reputation"'. Instead of seeking teachers they become apostolic acolytes within the hierarchy of whatever club they belong to; they are fashionable, cynical, and suspect everyone of fraudulence since they are fraudulent themselves. The delusion of clarity of insight pairs with sitting in judgement, a classical petty-god mentality masquerading as social responsibility and masking defensive and aggressive motivation.

A particular problem with dwelling in the head–breast compartment of lies in its plausibility. It is not so easy to tell the real thing from its imitation:

> The internal experience of these two mental acts, delusion-of-clarity-of-insight and sitting-in-judgement, seems to shade so subtly into their healthy counterparts, insight and judgement, that it is difficult to see how anything other than a widening of the field of introspection could distinguish them.
>
> ([1992] 2018, p. 83)

Meltzer calls this delusion of clarity of insight 'pseudo-maturity'.

Meanwhile the dwellers of the upper claustrum are generally disdainful of 'the sex-obsessed in the genital space and the dirty rascals in the rectum' whose disturbance is more evident. The genital dwellers are dominated by a 'primitive priapic religion' bearing a superficial resemblance to the ordinary adolescent world with its sexual preoccupations. But the adolescent is part of a group, and sex is psychologically secondary to social manoeuvrings which are 'more like a political party seeking a leader'. In psychic reality, looking from the outside, the parental bedroom is seen as

> a sanctum of mysterious and revered rites in which the father, with his penis and his semen nourishes, fertilises and cleanses the mother's procreative organs through all three of her major orifices. She is full of babies.
>
> ([1992] 2018, pp. 86–87)

The overarching vision is one in which love and work come together in the service of creativity, of all types. The genital dwellers (often themselves abused as children) have 'an absolute belief in the "irresistible" object and animal magnetism', leaving them on the verge of sadomasochism and degradation, in the face of either being or being in control of the phallus in the mother's body:

> Whether the burning desire is to *be* the irresistible phallus or to have absolute power over it, the essential object is the erect penis. All this is freely displayed and in the adolescent community passes undetected as a disturbance, for the 'over-the-top' ones are not shunned as in latency but admired.
>
> ([1992] 2018, p. 86)

This phantasy may hide under the guise of adolescent sexual experimentation. But anxieties emerge in the form of studying difficulties, feeding irregularities and obsessions.

In the adolescent community, although the bacchanale and orgy may be represented in group gatherings, it is symbolically – they do not literally devolve into group sex. The genital dweller however misses this distinction of symbol formation, owing to living in erotic concreteness, expressed in casual encounters and seductions:

> The phallus *as* fetish is a far cry from fetishism. While the feverish aspects of the sexual cravings of the genital cave-dweller do not bring him disapprobation but rather admiration from peers, he cannot escape the lingering sense of being an interloper amidst the joyousness of adolescent eroticism. Not only does he feel in imminent danger of being seduced over the border into perversity, but the need for multiple, transient and swift encounters makes a link with the essential feeling of treachery for the girl, in her secret oedipal triumph over a casual lover's wife; but feelings of cowardice for the boy in his evasion of competition, essentially oedipal, for his eye is always on the alert for the easy target and stereotyped sexiness. The consequence is the formation, analogous to the perverse subcommunity, of an erotomanic subcommunity of adolescents, stretching well into the thirties. By astute selection of targets for seduction and decisive sexual moves, they

both, male and female, arrange a satisfying confirmation of their phantasy of irresistibility.

([1992] 2018, pp. 87–88)

The young genital-dweller may thus escape unobserved for a crucial period of time, camouflaged by the normal adolescent 'joyous eroticism' whilst actually being carried on a perverse subterranean current under the tyrannical sway of the projected phallus.

It is however the rectal compartment of the Claustrum that is the most harmful. Whereas lodging in the head/breast or genital of the internal mother results in types of restricted immaturity, not incompatible with outwardly normal community life, imprisonment in the psychic rectum results in a catalogue of more evident social evils and internally in the type of fear designated by Bion as 'nameless dread' or by Meltzer as 'terror'. Meltzer explains its significance – the fear of being 'thrown away' (that is, outside the planetary system of the good internal objects):

> In essence we are dealing with the region of psychic reality where the atmosphere of sadism is pervasive and the hierarchic structure of tyranny and submission forebodes violence. For this reason, unlike the other two compartments where comfort and erotic pleasure dominate the value system, in the rectal compartment there is only one value: survival. Although the sadism may vary in intensity as one moves along the spectrum from boarding school to concentration camp, the atmosphere of incipient terror is probably little changed, for one meets evidence that the nameless dread consists in being 'thrown away'.
>
> ([1992] 2018, p. 88)

Seen from the outside, the rectum of the internal mother stores psychic rubbish produced by naughty children, ready to be cleansed by the internal father on the lines of the Augean Stables. Seen from the inside however, the 'great faecal penis' tyrannises over its concentration-camp prisoners, resulting in the degradation of values:

> Truth is transformed into anything that cannot be disproved; justice becomes talion plus an increment; all the acts of intimacy change their meaning into techniques of manipulation or dissimulation; loyalty replaces devotion; obedience substitutes for trust; emotion is simulated by excitement; guilt and the yearning for punishment takes the place of regret.
> ([1992] 2018, p. 89)

The ordinary fear of death is replaced by suicidal ruminations and the abuse of others. Meltzer explains that the faecal bad object is not actually an object at all 'but a self-object, compounded of a bad (disappointing, deserting) object and a cold (minus LHK) part of the self at part object level, therefore primitive'. It is a world without objects in the object relations or theological sense – the absence of God or gods. Meltzer says that this realisation does in face open up therapeutic possibilities 'for this great malignant object is potentially metabolisable into its component parts of self and object, dissolving the malignant character of the combination'. As Milton would put it, evil 'falls away'. But in practice this is not so easily achieved, partly because the individual may have caused actual harm to others, and partly because the Claustrum has its pleasures – additions, perversions and self-idealisations of a 'double agent' nature, whereby the rationale appears to be one of taking care of new recruits and teaching them the ropes so they can survive in a devious hierarchical system. Frantic ambition sets down a concrete ladder to 'the top', rationalised as the only safe place, even though it is well known how uneasy is the head that wears the crown.

As with all the chambers of the Claustrum, the perversion is often well disguised under the appearance of respectability, but in the rectal chamber, despair is ever-present – by contrast with the complacency of the ambitious head/breast dweller who is rarely assailed by any death instinct. Meltzer says that unlike the individual inhabiting other chambers, this one is often characterised by arousing fear in others:

> One of the puzzling features of this population, which one notices quite strongly in the analytic situation, is that they are frightening. They need not be big men. Quite small and fraillooking women can have it but it is difficult to simulate. How difficult for an actress to be a convincing Lady Macbeth. No, it is a mysterious charisma that paralyses the opposition. Somehow they are able to produce an atmosphere of hostage-holding, even if one cannot quite detect the identity of the hostage. It is always one's loved ones, in the last resort the children.
> ([1992] 2018, p. 92)

Ultimately, therefore, dwelling in any compartment of the Claustrum is anti-creative at best, murderous at worst.

It may be asked, what happens to the paternal object in this theory – which is predominantly built around the maternal internal object as container? Meltzer does not elaborate on this greatly here, since in terms of claustrophobic imprisonment, the male role is to be understood as essentially guarding the doorway to these internal spaces:

> The internal object of these processes is *par excellence* the internal maternal object and its special compartmentalisation. Where projection into the internal paternal object is obtrusive, it seems to be as a means of entry to the mother's body. It has important identificatory consequences but little of the claustrophobic, in its own right.
> ([1992] 2018, p. 57)

He differentiates dwelling in these compartments from other disturbances such as autism, the 'left behind' adolescents (as he terms them), or the 'unborn' still enwombed aspects of the personality – which nonetheless, the idea of the Claustrum helps us to understand better. These states are also different from what Money-Kyrle terms 'misconceptions'. Above all, this claustrophobic indwelling is sharply differentiated from imaginative venturing, which is dependent on an outside view of the inner world, and is richly illustrated by artists and poets.

The delusional system

There is a potential part or state of the personality which lies outside any relationship with these three object-related areas of the psyche. It is the delusional system, schizophrenia, madness itself. Meltzer (1979) writes: 'I would think that for most sane people, no part of the personality has, as yet, done more than have a peep into the delusional system at times of fever, intoxication – whatever'. He worked for many years with severely ill and schizophrenic patients but said that it was only possible to work with their non-delusional parts, not with the large area of the personality that had succumbed to delusion. In terms of internal geography, he regarded extreme projective or adhesive identification as bringing the personality to a kind of tipping-point beyond which it became lost to help and retrieval.

> In pitiful contrast to the glorious possibilities of growth for self and objects which the links of positive L, H and K embrace, the anti-life and anti-emotion forces which dedicate themselves to minus L, H and K – to puritanism, hypocrisy and philistinism – construct a Pandemonium of the delusional system. Their tools are stupid, essentially. Negative mimicry builds a world of delusional ideas and bizarre objects from the debris of alpha-function-in-reverse, aided by transformations in hallucinosis and the format of the Negative Grid.
> ([1992] 2018, p. 58)

It is the ultimate reach of the Negative Grid of anti-emotionality – Bion's 'alpha-function-in-reverse', running away from the personality structuring effected by symbol-formation, the aesthetic processing of emotional conflicts, that he regarded as superseding the theory of the life and death instincts. It is the 'nowhere' of the personality that feels it has been thrown out, devoid of meaning and value. Probably for Meltzer, however, there is always some tiny part of the personality still alive and reachable beneath the debris, just as the door to the Claustrum, he said, is always open.

Key text

Meltzer, D. ([1992] 2018). *The Claustrum*. London: Harris Meltzer Trust.

Chapter 6
Sexuality and creativity

The changing psychoanalytic approach to mental illness was traced by Money-Kyrle in terms of a move from sexual inhibitions, to moral conflict, and then to misconceptions. He saw these misconceptions as rooted in problems aroused during the very first cognitive life-situation: the link between mouth and nipple, which enables the phantasy of the parental intercourse. This link (rather than the body-ego) is the 'base' to which the ego orients itself – the 'O of the co-ordinate geometry of the mind' (Meltzer [1981] 2014, p. 240). His view is that most psychic problems can be seen in terms of a misconception of this primal scene, in which almost all variations are phantasised 'except the right one' – the right one being a creative intercourse. When in his paper on 'Cognitive development' (Money-Kyrle 1968) he writes of how his way of interpreting a dream of the parental intercourse has changed over the years, he in effect means *the* dream – the dream that underlies all others. It is one of three interlinked innate preconceptions – a good breast, a creative parental intercourse and death – that enable mental evolution, giving life meaning and structure. The 'psychic flow' of the mouth-and-nipple link (the container–contained that generates the internal 'combined object') is thus at the heart of the process of concept-building.

This was a concept with a prototype in Freud's 'superego ideal' which Meltzer said was primarily paternalistic, although at one point in *The Ego and the Id* Freud 'emphasises that what is internalised is a combination, a union of the original parental figures, and it is this union, this united or what Melanie Klein later calls "combined" object, that ... performs superego functions' and generates 'a sense of humility' ([1989] 2021, p. 23). Freud suggested it as a basis for non-narcissistic values, though not as a foundation for thinking and understanding reality, and Meltzer thought this aspect of Freud's picture of the superego was often forgotten by later adherents who made 'the dissolution of the superego into a therapeutic aim – most extraordinary'.

Money-Kyrle's view of the combined object as the source not only of values but also of thinking dovetails with that of Bion, whose theory of maternal reverie and alpha-function clarifies how the first feeding experiences can be understood in terms of thinking processes, not just physical needs or gratification (as indeed is known to mothers and to students of infant observation). The overriding dynamic is the search for truth, by 'learning from experience'; though where Bion sees this search as deflected by lies and basic assumptions, Money-Kyrle sees it as clouded by misconceptions. Our moral or ethical failures derive from our perceptual defects, rather than the other way round. And he does mean *defects*, not merely differences – which ultimately means defects in our vision of the creative parental intercourse of the 'combined object'.

Meltzer's revised theory of sexuality, set out in *Sexual States of Mind* (1973), in a sense combines the three phases of the psychoanalytic approach. Sexuality, ethics and thought processes are intimately connected. Although we no longer speak in terms of normal and deviant, sane and healthy, this does not mean there are no values, no distinction between good and bad. On the contrary, the unconscious phantasy life expressed in sexuality, that has its roots in infancy, is intimately connected with cognitive development and thinking. However in discussing sexual states he is focusing primarily not on sexual actions but on sexual phantasy, as it appears in the consulting room, in dreams in particular. And he makes a crucial and novel distinction between adult and infantile sexuality as fluctuating mental states that are not tied to phases of life but relate to internal psychic organisation and the dynamics of the depressive and paranoid-schizoid positions.

Sexual states are key to the individual's sense of identity. Meltzer emphasises that he is looking at psychological states rather than external behaviour or cultural values; yet the knowledge gained in the consulting room has applications way beyond it, in the outside world. Since our multiform sexuality governs the way we learn and hence the way we teach, there are implications for teaching methods at particular stages of child development, which he describes in a chapter on 'Pedagogic implications of structural psychosexual theory' in *Sexual States*. In the process he also offers an entirely new perspective on abortion which is neither prescriptively religious nor mechanical, and yet has still not found its way into society's norms.

Infantile sexual states of mind

Meltzer begins his review, as always, by summarising the historical conception, first separating Freud's conception of infantile sexuality as polymorphously perverse into polymorphism and perversity. This enables an exploration of problems of narcissistic organisation, and a new view of perversions, addictions, fetishism and regressive illness in general. In the realms of sexuality, as in other aspects, the psychoanalytic model moves from a hydraulic one based on the flow of energy (the libido theory) to one of communication in which 'the thrust toward development rather than the minimising of tension is seen as the ultimate economic principle' ([1973] 2018, p. 22).

A major shift in perception comes with the work of Abraham (Klein's analyst), whose scheme of the stages in sexual development is summarised by Meltzer as: early and late oral stages, early and late anal sadistic stages, and early and late genital or phallic stages. It remained schematic until the psychoanalytic method was adapted for work with children; before that, there was no realistic picture of the intense conflicts and anxieties undergone by children in their efforts to 'strengthen the goodness of the internal objects on whom they must, during separation and eventually, totally, depend for support' ([1973] 2018, p. 40). Indeed the creativity of small children he saw as first expressed by a well-formed stool, a 'gift of love' to the mother, demonstrating inner patience and readiness.

In order to achieve the separation and introjection of good objects children need to learn to move from a 'pain and fear' orientation (self-protective) to one of 'love and pain' – to overriding concern for the object, the depressive position proper. This is governed by what was originally called in Freudian terms the super-ego-ideal, then later in Kleinian terms, the combined object, and forms the basis for 'adult sexuality' in Meltzer's definition, which is not age-restricted. For overriding all phantasy states is the picture of the primal scene as the governing frame of reference for sexual states of mind both adult and infantile: a scene which may be phantasised in an entire spectrum of ways.

Within the infantile category, Meltzer differentiates infantile polymorphous sexuality, a fluctuating state, from the infantile perversity that can infiltrate adult life. Polymorphous sexuality is egocentric, masturbatory and tends toward 'wanton as distinct from compulsive promiscuity', being essentially experimental. It strongly characterises adolescence but also small children, expressing a sense of puzzlement about the nature of genuine creativity. Far more prevalent in the psychoanalytic consulting room is evidence of perverse infantile sexuality, dominated by the weak or sadistic superego which is sometimes reinforced by an actual parent–child relationship. However Meltzer explains that the use of terms such as homosexual, heterosexual, transvestite, fellatio, fetishism and lesbian are descriptive with regard to sexual acts or leanings, but do not classify states of mind in a psychoanalytic sense. Of the traditional terminology, 'only "sadistic" and "masochistic" find a place in a psychoanalytical classification' ([1973] 2018, p. 115).

Adolescence

All times of crisis and crucial points of development are regulated by the interplay of the paranoid-schizoid and depressive positions. In Meltzer's summary: sexuality is in abeyance during the protective period of latency, in which the child can focus on acquiring skills and information in the outside world, and erupts again owing to biological pressures in puberty.

> In puberty it seems the organisation of the personality that had been built up during the first ten or eleven years of life suddenly reveals itself to be very fragile, falls to pieces and has to be newly constructed, intensifying the obsessional mechanisms. Thus in the transition from latency to puberty we can see a continuous oscillation in behaviour between that of a turbulent child and of a self-contained adult, in close sequence.
> (Meltzer & Harris [2011] 2018, p. 115)

It is in the adolescent, owing to these biological changes and the related resurgence of infantile confusions, that 'the problem of identity is most in evidence'. The adolescent, unlike the child, lives more in the adolescent community than in the family, and finds containment there in the sense of a space to work through the 'potpourri' of fluctuating sexual states of mind ranging from adult to infantile – the sense of identity at times being held by the adult part but never for long. The general direction is from the world of childhood to the pubertal homosexual group then to the adolescent heterosexual group. Zonal and geographical confusions come to a head at this archetypal period of crisis: in the context of problems of differentiation between good and bad, between self and object, the Oedipus complex, and above all, the differentiation of the adult part from the infantile part of the personality.

> One has the impression that in this phase of development processes of intense disintegration are repeated, typical of the

paranoid-schizoid position, which from the point of view of dynamics link to the time just after weaning.

([1973] 2018, p. 115)

Meltzer categorises four types of adolescent: the adolescent who remains within the family in an extension of the latency period, often establishing their own family early in a type of unreal fairytale that is liable later to break down; the rigidly ambitious adolescent who aims too rapidly to enter the adult world; the isolated adolescent who retreats into his own narcissistic organisation and is most seriously at risk; and the suffering adolescent who is aware of their own difficulties and moves or fluctuates between all these modes of existence.

> Essentially, the adolescent group is extremely safe and very healthy; the adolescent can have his experiences accompanied by suffering, but there is no risk of fixation or catastrophe, unless adults impose restrictions which drive the group towards negativism.
>
> ([1973] 2018, p. 66)

For the adolescent in therapy, who generally belongs to either the isolated or the suffering group, it is important to evaluate their degree of tolerance of suffering – 'the level of depressive pain that he is able to tolerate in relation to confusion'. Awareness of confusion is the necessary foundation of the search for an authentic identity.

One of the corollaries of distinguishing different qualities of pain and confusion concerns the psychic reality of unborn children and thus the problem of abortion. In Meltzer's view the baby is always psychically the mother's alone (not the father's nor society's), but the physical pregnancy may not have been apprehended in psychic reality; and even if it has, there is a difference between the baby being experienced introjectively as the mother's own (in which case mourning is possible), or experienced through projective identification as the internal mother's possession, in which case, following an abortion, 'the gateway to regressive illness is opened wide' ([1973] 2018, p. 200).

The perversions and addictions

Meltzer also differentiates within the category of perversion, which he says is not adequately accounted for by the contrast between narcissistic and object-related states. Fetish formation is ubiquitous in the perversions proper, defined as 'the sado-masochistic game with which an addictive attachment can be formed'; it is not merely narcissistic but mechanical in its autoerotic level of sensuality which 'precludes emotionality, memory or satisfaction':

> Where dependence on internal good objects is rendered infeasible by damaging masturbatory attacks and where dependence on a good external object is unavailable or not acknowledged, the addictive relationship to a bad part of the self, the submission to tyranny, takes place. An illusion of safety is promulgated by the omniscience of the destructive part and perpetuated by the sense of omnipotence generated by the perversion or addictive activity involved.
> ([1973] 2018, p. 125)

Internal tyrannical states therefore result in perversions and addictions (as in the Claustrum). The autoerotic nature accounts for its socialised form, 'the you-do-it-to-me and then I'll-do-it-to-you' aspect. Meltzer sees an analogy here with political tyranny as a social perversion whose ultimate form is war – the murder of the mother's internal babies. Such states begin when the imprisoned narcissistic self retreats from the turbulence of the impact of the beauty of the world (internal and external) which is manifest or created by this internal combined object. It tries to maintain omnipotent control, and substitutes a self-object for a real one.

When manifest in a clinical situation, this tends to a 'perversion of the transference'. The central phantasy is terror of the internal dead babies.

Creativity and the adult state of mind

By contrast with the multiplicity of infantile sexual states, the adult sexual state of mind can be simply described. Essentially it is when the sense of identity is governed by a phantasy of creative internal objects who require useful work in the service of the world-as-mother. For Meltzer describes adult sexuality as a form of work, rather than explaining work as a sublimation of sexuality as in the earlier psychoanalytic model, which is 'really a kind of trickiness by which the person manages to attain gratification in a disguised and devious way that escapes either the disapproval of the community or the severity of the superego' ([1989] 2021, p. 23).

As throughout, he is not focussing on literal sexual relationships (though these overlap) but on the internal phantasy of a creative combined object, as in Money-Kyrle's definition of the essential preconception that in his patients (he said) he almost always found to be wrong. This wrong idea of internal creativity can be considered to be at the root of all psychic disturbance. His psychological model is internally, not socially, based, though it has social consequences. Its ethics derive from a picture of the internal couple and the fostering and protection of internal babies. The internal combined object is by definition bisexual, and this bisexuality governs the adult sense of identity when it is fully integrated:

> It is clear that the adult sense of identity derives from the introjective identification with parental figures and is fundamentally bisexual, although an individual's integration may not have proceeded so far as to enable bisexuality to be experienced and acknowledged.
> ([1973] 2018, p. 99)

The picture of the mind in this integrated state sheds a new light on the concept of the depressive position and its traditional Kleinian ethic of reparation, focussing on a sense of responsibility for the internal mother's 'babies' in all their representations:

> The depressive position tends toward the externalisation of the combined internal object on to wider and wider representation in the outside world, finally taking the form of equating the earth and sun with the parents, so that all the humans alive come to represent the mother's children, siblings, while the animal life and the dead represent her 'internal babies'.
> ([1973] 2018, p. 144)

In later Klein, as in Bion, the paranoid-schizoid and depressive positions lose their original tie to phases of infant development, and are seen to apply throughout life in a perpetual oscillation. Reparation cannot be done actively by the omnipotent baby-self but only by the object, if the 'baby' restrains its destructive impulses: 'Reparation comes to be the precise opposite of destructive impulses and is connected very directly with the concept of integration' (Meltzer & Harris [2011] 2018, p. 108).

The reparative phantasy applies not only to literal human babies but to animal, plant and environmental life – the riches of fertile mother earth, the object of our apprehension of beauty. The adult part of the personality assumes a sense of responsibility for the world; and personality development entails infantile parts growing out of their egocentric values and moving in the direction of adult parts with their depressive values. This is not dependent on external sexual allegiances/gender orientation or actions but on internal ones where everyone is bisexual and lives under the aegis of a 'combined object'. Nor is it dependent on the age or developmental phase of the individual; some babies can be more in touch with their adult part than their literal parents.

It is this model or picture which justifies Meltzer's view that sublimation is insufficient, indeed irrelevant, to creative activity of all kinds. Rather, under the aegis of the combined object, adult sexuality (in the sense of the phantasy of the combined object) has the meaning of work. Not just work towards personal identity and self-knowledge, but work in the sense of useful activity in the world, on behalf of 'all the babies':

> Depressive concern for 'all the mother's babies' tends to express itself in acts which not only have the meaning of reparation, in the sense of Melanie Klein, but also of an activity which I have called 'sermonising' and recognised as the motive force behind the 'publication' (in Bion's sense) of works of art and science.
>
> ([1973] 2018, p. 144)

In conclusion: 'The integrated internal combined object learns from experience in advance of the self and is almost certainly the fountainhead of creative thought and imagination' ([1992] 2018, p. 58). On the basis of clinical experience, he considered this internalisation to be a 'rare phenomenon' (2005c, p. 180). Meltzer believed that, in practice, the adult state of mind is at its most stable during the life period when families are literally being raised; and that when children have flown the nest there is a much greater chance of retreat to the adolescent 'pot-pourri' of fluctuating sexual modalities. Nonetheless this social viewpoint is not essential to the psychoanalytic basis of his post-Kleinian model, which is led by his vision of the combined object in a parallel way to Bion's model being led by 'intersection with O', the ultimate fount of wisdom and contact with reality.

Artistic creativity he believed to have a special place in this overall vision: 'Creativity does not require that there should be an integration of the self, but that there should be an integrated combined object well internalised'. In this context, he stressed the extreme difficulty of maintaining the adult state – the integrated object – suggesting that artists often need to split their personal lives (their selves) from the heightened state that he calls 'sermonising to siblings', in which they are dominated by the sense of being used by internal objects for purposes of educating the world:

> Creativity is a term which has special reference to artists. While development involves some give-and-take with objects, creativity comes with a strong feeling of being used by internal objects as a medium to relay knowledge to the world – communication, mission, preaching to siblings.
>
> (2005c, pp. 179–180)

In order to survive this heightened obligation to objects, using his special talent for symbolisation, the artist may lead his everyday life at a lower level of ethics and mental health:

> A creative genius is someone who permits his own internal objects to give him new ideas – even if he does not understand them or cannot use them; his function is to receive them, and he possesses the art of transmitting them. There is a distinction between invention and discovery. Invention is a function of the self; discovery, a function of the creative self.
>
> (2005c, p. 175)

This then is Meltzer's view of the difference between artistic functioning and personality development. The artist, the scientist, and perhaps the psychoanalyst 'function at a higher level than they function in their own family'. They may not even personally benefit from the knowledge which they mediate on behalf of others. Essentially however it is not a difference in type but a difference in degree, moving from depressive concern for the object to servicing the object's instructions, even if blind to their significance – something akin to religious faith. All development is governed by internal objects who are themselves allowed to develop in creative conjunction; and this, according to Meltzer, depends upon establishing the compartmentalisation of the internal mother, which is 'the precondition for the evolution of qualities of mind of these parental figures, extrapolating to the infinity of truthfulness, goodness and wisdom – to godhead' ([1992] 2018, p. 65).

Nobody can maintain constantly an 'adult' mode of sexuality; nonetheless this striving towards dependence on the internal 'combined object' underlies the 'quest for wisdom', in a constant oscillation between paranoid-schizoid and depressive positions which entails (internally) 'permanent revolution, not only in July and October but every day' ([1973] 2018, p. 185).

Key text

Meltzer, D. ([1973] 2018). *Sexual States of Mind.* London: Harris Meltzer Trust.

Part II

Life in the consulting room

Chapter 7

The aesthetics of the process

The analytical process is a 'natural product' of the structure of the mind ([1967] 2018, p. xviii). The method and the model of the mind are interdependent, and gradually evolve to become more sophisticated, in response to clinical observation. Beauty accrues not only to the mind but also to the method by which its workings become manifest and which has its own 'aesthetic' (Meltzer & Williams [1988] 2018, p. 25).

When psychoanalysis evolved from a medical science to an art-science, the original model of diagnosis and treatment became gradually superseded by a different view of how therapeutic results might be achieved. This depended far more on the analyst's own introspection and example, through active engagement with the patient in the transference. Instead of correct interpretation being considered the main therapeutic tool, a more complex interpretive network was envisaged, on the lines of thinking aloud in the presence of the patient, or rather, in conversation with their internal objects. Direct or judgemental interpretation could be relegated to the realms of 'action', that is, trying to impose an action upon the patient. By contrast, the analytical conversation comes to focus on communication and exploration. Meltzer says the analyst is constantly faced with a choice between these two modes of interpretation and needs to be aware of the temptation to verbally act, which is usually the result of a failure to contain the anxiety of not-knowing. For as he put it at the end of his first book, in the chapter on 'Psychoanalysis as a human activity', it is a 'serious question how anyone can practise analysis without being damaged' ([1967] 2018, p. 97).

Meltzer said that the purpose of psychoanalysis was to 'strike fire' in the mind of the patient ([1997] 2021, p. 113 – a metaphor also used by Bion and Jung). He does not cease to stress the need for vitality on the part of the analyst as probably the most essential requirement. To this, the theories employed and even the model (so much wider and more imaginative than the theory) are secondary. When an analyst gets to the stage of having seen it all before, knowing what it's all about, etc., it is better if they retire. Both Bion and Meltzer compare the analyst entering the consulting room on a new day to the baby being born: it is essential to retain the capacity for 'surprise' that accompanies every chance of illumination. There is a natural tendency to retreat from this propulsion that Meltzer compared to Freud's formulation of 'psychic inertia', something which 'so opposes growth that an input of vitality in the form of analytic determination is required during the working through periods' ([1973] 2018, p. 86).

For Meltzer, 'every psychoanalytical discovery is a self-revelation and every paper an autobiography' ([1973] 2018, p. xiii). Like Bion, he was very conscious of the extent to which every analysis is an opportunity for continuation of the analyst's self-analysis. This of course depends on alertness to the countertransference, a phenomenon which was originally documented only in the sense of 'acting out' on the part of the analyst, and thus a hindrance (like transference, on its first discovery), until it was understood that (like projective identification) there was another type of countertransference which was in fact essential to the vitality of the psychoanalytic relationship, being the only way the analyst can register an emotional response and thereby investigate it.

Meltzer also regretted the increasing difficulty of publishing clinical work, which he felt the only way (outside personal supervision) to share genuine experiences in the field in any wide or international way. For in his own view, if presented truthfully, clinical work was indeed autobiography, not failure of confidentiality: autobiography which expressed a respectful interest in the patient as the leader in the investigation. He pointed out that he had been written about by Mrs Klein and felt 'a great honour',[1] but was aware that not all his patients felt the same way (2000b, p. 161).

Psychoanalysis he regarded as a 'beautiful method' by which two people could have 'the most interesting conversation in the world, hour by hour, for years, and to relinquish it with regret owing to the imperative of psychic reality' (Meltzer & Williams [1988] 2018, p. xxi) – that imperative being the need for separation so the analysand can fully internalise the experience and continue through self-analysis. He compared it to watching the shadows on the wall of Plato's cave. You never find out 'the truth' in a factual sense because psychoanalysis is not like an archaeological dig, a reconstruction on the lines of the 'lawyer or the sleuth'; it is a present, live communication between minds: 'The good news is that you don't have to pay any attention to the patient's history; and the bad news, that you have to pay a lot of attention to what goes on in the consulting room' ([2000a] 2021, p. 117).

Meltzer's final definition of psychoanalysis was 'a conversation between internal objects'. The container for this conversation is not the mind of the analyst, nor indeed the mind of the patient, but the link between them (as in Bion), a mysterious phenomenon that is supported by the analytic process itself, which he viewed as an art form – something which precludes 'respectability' since aesthetic impact relies on evocation and reciprocity (Meltzer & Williams [1988] 2018, p. xx). When the links are, as Bion would say, not too slack and not too tense, there is a chance for the different perspectives or vertices to get into constructive interchange. This is not the same as intersubjectivity; rather, it is a meeting of minds which together form a container by means of what Bion calls 'fit':

> The model of container–contained places a new value on receptiveness and the holding of the dynamic situation of transference–countertransference in the mind. But perhaps to state this as if the analyst were the container misses the point that it is the fitting together of the analyst's attention and attitudes to the cooperativeness of the patient that forms and seals the container, lending it the degree of flexibility and resilience required from moment to moment.
>
> ([1986] 2018, p. 250)

The defensive operations which psychoanalysis is designed to follow may now be seen as 'moves against the impact of the aesthetic object' – the analysis itself, rather than the person of the analyst – and this results in refinements of the method. Symbol formation may be resisted for this very reason – it 'captures feelings and gives them a form', which may be experienced as 'cruelly restrictive' (in Williams [2010] 2018, p. 106).

In the 'Denouement' to *Studies in Extended Metapsychology,* Meltzer reviews his ideas on this post-Kleinian development, which he associates with the gradual introjection of Bion's ideas. The first and most important change is 'a diminished emphasis on the "correctness" of interpretation' which 'loses its explanatory function' and instead the focus moves forwards into 'the interaction, the relationship from which interpretive ideas emerge'. The function, and therefore framing, of the analyst's own words is descriptive rather than diagnostic, something Meltzer compares to a guide shining a light on a wall of cave-paintings, shifting the angle so that different images become visible, ultimately linking together into a frieze.

> This image of the analyst's verbal task, to shine a light of understanding from one vertex after another, modifies the

atmosphere of communication to an extraordinary degree, diminishing the authoritarian expectations of the patient and sharing the responsibility between the members of the work group of two. It also allows an interpretive line gradually to form. Certain dreams – the dreams and not their interpretations – establish the landmarks for both members.

([1986] 2018, p. 250)

Again, he uses an analogy from art to describe how a picture of the containing object can be gradually formed within an analysis, as a result of the analytic process taking on a new 'shape' and being seen as an aesthetic 'thing-in-itself':

This has far-reaching implications for the transference and countertransference for it establishes an object upon which are not imposed, in Freud's terms, the limitations inherent in the 'particularities' of the analyst – his age, sex, appearance, known facts about his life situation, his values, politics, etc. In fact it allows for the formation of an object which the therapist and patient can examine together from a certain distance, in the same way that one steps back from most paintings to allow the composition to impinge, and then steps forward to appreciate the brush strokes and craftsmanship.

([1986] 2018, p. 251)

The vision of psychoanalysis as aesthetic object always characterised Meltzer's approach, but Bion's concept of the 'catastrophic change' that always heralds a new idea enabled the method and the model of the mind to come into focus as the 'new idea' of psychoanalysis:

The 'new idea' was clearly something like: 'In the beginning was the aesthetic object, and the aesthetic object was the breast and the breast was the world.' Of course I am using the word 'breast' as a technical term with only an implication of description, rather than the other way round.

([1986] 2018, pp. 244–245)

Looking back over his own influences, Meltzer lists Klein, Stokes, Bion, as well as his own work with the dreams of patients and the artwork of centuries. All these contributed to formulating the new idea of the psychoanalytic process as aesthetic object which had been latent in his work from early on.

> Not only had I become aware that the psychoanalytical method had taken on an aesthetic quality in my eyes but I had begun to see, mainly through dreams, that it had done so for some of my patients as well.
>
> ([1986] 2018, p. 244)

The new idea was, in fact, an old idea with light shone upon it from a different angle. And this had practical implications, not merely philosophical ones.

It is toleration of the 'situation of uncertainty', the state of unknowing, that enables the analyst to be receptive to the essential nature of psychoanalysis as aesthetic object, providing a means of searching for the truth but never of possessing it:

> This permits us to formulate better the nature of the passionate contact which is propelled by K (the K-link) – the wish to understand that allows us to hold together the turbulence of love and hate. It permits us also to formulate more precisely a method for modulating the anxiety produced by catastrophic change, whose destructive impact would otherwise pull the mind towards the negative grid, that is, towards lies and negativity … Even if you don't always succeed in understanding the internal state of the patient, the analyst should nonetheless be under the dominance of K, that is, of the desire to understand.
>
> (2005c, pp. 178–179)

This very uncertainty, the awareness of watching the shadows on the wall of the cave – never the sun directly – protects the mind from lies and false knowledge, so long as the anxiety can be tolerated.

The setting and the task

It is the psychoanalytic setting that enables transference processes to find expression, and this has become refined over the years in terms of recognising the need to avoid social relations with the patient and other personal features that interfere with transference. Meltzer, unlike Bion, emphasises the setting and gives it very specific importance. He stresses that it is nothing to do with institutional regulations about five times a week and other 'political problems' that are in essence not scientific. Rather, it is to do with creating a space in which 'showing it' can lead over 'saying it'; for the analytical process has 'a momentum of its own and finds a means of expression that goes beyond words'. This matter of 'private definition' can then be translated into 'public presentation' for discussion with colleagues.

In practical terms, each analyst must, through experience, come up with their own ideas about the setting and their own technique, and consequently what counts as a breach of technique. And this may vary with the individual patient. Always the dynamics of the process depend on the oscillation of the paranoid-schizoid and depressive positions, given the notation Ps↔D by Bion: a dynamic which the rhythm of separations is designed to bring into focus, modulating its pain and promoting the capacity for love:

> This delicate balance between progression and regression exists at every step in the growth process. It forms, in the dimension of time, a spiral configuration of no great geometrical regularity. This oscillation is studied with compelling force in the four time units of psychoanalysis, the session, the week, the term and the year, punctuated by the separation units (night, week-end, holiday, summer break).
>
> ([1973] 2018, p. 203)

Within this conception of rhythmic process, however, the analyst should be 'flexible with regard to frequency, duration of sessions, spacing, missing of sessions or periods of therapy, methods of payment, use of the couch, bringing or sending of written or graphic materials, interviews with relatives' ([1986] 2018, p. 253). There is no point rigidly insisting on preset rules of procedure, since if kept under careful scrutiny by the analyst, a rational flexibility can have a 'humanising and encouraging effect'.

Maintenance of the setting is important also for the analyst's own development and self-observation, given that the most 'fundamental unit' of the setting is an 'inner qualification', namely 'the state of mind of the analyst' ([1967] 2018, p. 84). In order to strenuously preserve the psychoanalytic attitude the analyst must constantly review his procedures and 'promote his own learning from experience' ([1986] 2018, p. 253). The analyst's efforts to resist countertransference activity are based on self-awareness; 'modulation of anxiety on the one hand and the minimising of interference on the other' requires a 'constant process of discovery', that is, self-discovery. He clarifies what he means by 'modulation' of anxiety:

> Note that the term 'modulation' of anxiety has been used rather than 'modification', since the latter is surely a function of the interpretive aspect of the work while the modulation is managed as part of the setting. This modulation occurs through the patient's repeated experience in analysis that there is a place where the expression of his transference processes will not be met by countertransference activity but only by analytical activity, namely a search for the truth.
>
> ([1967] 2018, p. xviii)

Modulation is a feature of the setting, in Meltzer's special usage. Its prime aim is not to ease anxiety but to seek truth, a joint venture of the transference – communication rather than action. Ultimately, the analyst's interpretive activity will 'contribute to the patient's capacity for insight' – but only if it is genuinely part of a personal process of discovery.

The doing, and the talking about, psychoanalysis, are 'different functions', with different modes of interpretation – expressive or explanatory. There needs to be an interchange between immersion in the countertransference dream (being 'lost' in the process) and 'surfacing' to take stock of what has been learned, whether in supervision or in personal reflection. For, unlike other sciences, 'each analyst, guided by teachers and the literature, must "discover" the whole of analysis for himself':

> Until the analyst's experience is wide on the one hand and his character has been stabilised by analytic treatment on the other, this structure of theory is continually toppling down under the stress of analytic work, its pain, confusion, worry, guilt, disappointment. The 'surfacing' to take stock, which occurs while the student is in analysis and while the young analyst is having supervision, must eventually be taken over as an autonomous process.
>
> ([1967] 2018, p. xxii)

Through this interchange, there gradually develops a 'research capacity'. By this Meltzer does not mean academic research but the personal observation and organization of 'psychoanalytic phenomena beyond the verification of all [the young analyst] has been taught' (p. xxiii). He felt however that there can well be a price to pay, without sufficiently strong internal objects; and to avoid the pitfalls of either complacency or personal harm, the analyst needs to keep himself psychically 'in racehorse condition' (p. 98). And by 'damage' he means not psychosis, but 'failure of development', which can be damaging to other workers also (p. 100).

For the analyst has 'the same type of aesthetic conflict in their love affair with the psychoanalytical method' as does the patient, or any person, engaged in a developmental experience. Love, hate and the desire for knowledge are engaged in the turbulence of catastrophic change (in Bion's term). In facilitating the growth of new ideas, through the analytic relationship, the analyst's capacity depends upon 'his ability to free himself from concern with the past and future of the relationship and his tolerance of the catastrophic anxiety he would need to share with the patient' ([1978] 2018, vol. 3, p. 125) – Bion's advocacy of eschewing memory and desire.

Meltzer always considers the advance of psychoanalysis as a group effort; but he differentiates the passionate experience of the individual analyst following the method from the basic assumption pressures (Bion) both within the profession and externally in society:

> Clearly the method, with its intimacy, privacy, ethics, attentiveness, forbearance, non-judgemental stance, its continuity, open-endedness, implicit readiness for sacrifice on the analyst's part, commitment to recognise errors, sense of responsibility towards the patient and his family all of which is embodied in the dedication to scrutinise the transference–countertransference process – all of these facets, bound together by systematic effort, make the method unequivocally an aesthetic object. But within the method is the theory by which it is practised, and this theory is notoriously open to suspicion; among the list of often mutually exclusive accusations which have been levelled against it, one may include those of being reductionist, bourgeois, cynical, simplistic, hypocritical, unscientific, messianic, satanic, antiChristian, paternalistic, mechanistic, sexist, antisexual, amoral, moralistic.
>
> (Meltzer & Williams [1988] 2018, p. 23)

The natural history of the process

Meltzer saw a developmental pattern as inherent in the psychoanalytic method. Any psychoanalysis, if carried through to a proper ending, follows the 'natural history' of the process, as set out in his first book *The Psychoanalytical Process* ([1967] 2018, p. 5): that is, a logical developmental thread equivalent to an organic growth. This comprises five main phases: the gathering of the transference, the sorting of geographical confusions, the sorting of zonal confusions, the threshold of the depressive position and the weaning process. Each of these phases depends upon work done in the previous phase, that cannot be bypassed 'since each phase has an absolute metapsychological dependence on the adequate working-through of the previous one' (p. 36). Meltzer delineated this picture in *The Psychoanalytical Process*, which was mainly based on work with children, but he saw it as applicable to adults also, just more clearly visible in children. The behavioural description is different but the structural implications are the same. The goal is to establish dependence on internal primal good objects, by means of the external dependence on the analytic setting and process.

A psychoanalysis begins with establishing a transference relationship on the lines of the infantile transference to the mother, parent, object. The 'analytic situation', as Mrs Klein called it, means 'the situation into which the transferences of a person's life are sucked, rather like a vacuum-cleaner; it can be called "the gathering of the transference"' (2000b, p. 2). Yet as described above, this cannot be established without first overcoming the preformed transference and dismissing it from the consulting room – a task that can be difficult and time-consuming with adults, but is necessary to avoid a fake analytic situation.

Following this, geographical confusions make themselves known through 'massive projective identification' (a term later revised to 'intrusive identification'), blurring the boundaries between self and object in the transference. This is intensified during separations. The first part-object to become valued, though not loved, is what Meltzer terms the 'toilet-breast', which functions initially through splitting off the 'feeding-breast':

> Before the internal 'toilet-breast' has been established the unavailability of an object in the outside world capable of containing such pain throws the ego back on massive projective

identification with an internal object: if this fails to control the anxiety, states of schizophrenic withdrawal into delusion or autistic fragmentation, separately or in tandem, appear to be the only recourse.

([1967] 2018, p. 26)

When the toilet-breast is established, there will be a 'dearth of depressive anxieties' within the analysis owing to splitting, while good things are experienced as existing elsewhere in life. In children this phase is manifest graphically in dirtying playroom behaviour; in adults geographical confusion is associated with the 'pseudo-mature' personality, a fake identification with the good breast. In adolescents it may take the form of missing sessions and delinquency. As the split becomes less rigid, allowing the emergence of 'severe anxieties of soiling, polluting and poisoning the feeding-breast', which the analyst can help to modulate:

> While almost endless patience – and tolerance – may be required of the analyst in this phase, progress is almost always steadily achieved. The patient who cannot manage it will either break down at a holiday or leave before or after one.
> ([1967] 2018, p. 24)

It is a phase rather than an 'intractable resistance' and, as such, may be overcome simply by persevering with the analytic method, enabling greater tolerance of psychic pain. (These more intractable states of geographical confusion are dealt with in detail later in *The Claustrum.*) As its dominance lessens, 'the mid-week begins to clear' but is liable to return in force at breaks and holidays.

As one anti-developmental phase or state loses its grip, the next is revealed and may be worked on, initially in the mid-week and mid-term hours which are the 'central analytic period' less disturbed by separation anxieties. The Oedipus complex appears, muddled in genital and pre-genital forms, a 'confusion of zones and modes' (a term he says is borrowed from Erikson, and descriptive of unconscious phantasy rather than of instincts). It is characterised by a search for gratification of all sorts, a state of excitement. At this time the playroom or consulting room changes from being either 'inside' or 'outside' and becomes 'the place of analysis', a work-space of its own (p. 26). This phase is dominated by 'desire and jealousy, rather than by the struggle against the experience of separateness'. The analytic work consists in attempting to lessen omnipotence by demonstrating the anxieties consequent on its function. From a countertransference point of view 'the constant resisting of seduction and aggression can be fatiguing and the violence of the passions rather alarming' (p. 29). Splitting of the toilet-mummy is intensified and the analyst is contemptuously regarded as a mere receptacle for pain, while the self is in possession of the beautiful part-objects. A confusion of the sensuality of the various zones and their corresponding objects encourages a type of 'quasi-aesthetic appreciation'. Gradually this confusion is de-idealised as narcissism is curtailed, and an approach can be begun to be severely denied and split-off introjective dependence on the object.

Acting-out requires partners, whether siblings, friends or spouses; but as with the geographical stage, this phase rarely encounters 'intractable resistance' unless it is part of an established pattern of delinquency, perversion or addiction. Meltzer's message is always, 'if the analyst can persevere':

> At the 'threshold of the depressive position' it can be seen that the growth of actual dependence and the growth of its acknowledgement proceed independently, the projective relation to the mother (toilet-breast) being more easily established than the introjective (feeding-breast) ... This in turn is more easily accepted than the necessary role of the paternal penis.
> ([1967] 2018, p. 36)

It is a shock to the analyst to discover that not trust but distrust comes to the fore during this phase – distrust in 'the analyst's own strength and adequacy as a good breast': not 'I don't need you' but 'You are not what I need'. 'From denial to negation, in Freud's terms'. The world has improved but the patient becomes uneasy about the analyst's health and vitality. Meltzer denotes this the 'latency period' of the analytic process, a deceptive quietude directed to the outside world and liable to be astounded by the shock of emotional turbulence when it surfaces. At this stage the analyst's fighting spirit must be called into play, more than his capacity to bear pain as in the earlier stages; for despite appearances, 'the security of the internal world has *not* been established and termination is unthinkable'. The destructive infantile part 'fights a last-ditch stand' with cynical attacks on the truth and the aggravation of depressive anxieties. Typical themes here are: 'parents abandon their children to indulge sexually and analysts abandon their patients at weekends and holidays'; 'out-of-sight is out-of-mind'; parents and analysts only look after their children/patients because they must, from law and custom, to preserve their respectability; the parent–child or analyst–patient alliance is just a tyrannical class structure; parental roles are rationalised despotism; parents and analysts don't really love their children or they would keep them 'happy'; beauty and goodness never win out in the struggle with evil. Meltzer stresses that this last may appear true in the external world, but not in psychic reality, and is the foundation of vitality, joy and security.

Indeed this phase is characterised by attacks on the analytic setting: 'the analyst is continually put to the test of clarifying, for himself and his patient, the rationale of the setting, demeanour and mechanics of communication' (p. 40). Yet destructive parts are kept split off, thus 'represented in dream, play and association by figures other than the self', a rationalised possessiveness by the 'good' infantile part. Fear of being bullied by the destructive parts is heightened and there may be panic around psychosomatic symptoms. Again the mid-week work contrasts with the infantile dominance around the breaks. 'At no time is the concreteness of splitting processes more starkly evident'. The central force opposing integration is infantile possessive jealousy and greed: integration requiring, at the infantile level, the sharing of good object; and at the adult level, responsibility for psychic reality. Love of the breast and its beauty exists, but not the strength to defend it, which requires trust (gratitude, in Klein's term); this occurs gradually through a 'repeated rhythmic experience of destruction and restoration, of despair and hope, of mental pain and joy':

> As the depressive position is penetrated more deeply, the threshold problem of being able to accept forgiveness *by* good objects for attacks and defections becomes replaced by the problem of being able to *forgive oneself* for past breaches of good faith. This, along with the genital Oedipus complex, forms the central theme of the phase of weaning or termination.
>
> ([1967] 2018, p. 44)

The gradual acquirement of ego-strength is indicated in dreams such as those of an adolescent girl, at times of separation, learning to control the 'manic wave' imaged in wild car driving and to clean her own psychological bottom, as imaged in a dream of fingerpostcards addressed to 'M. T. Brown' (emptying of faeces). The second dream shows 'the identification in her adult self with the analyst-mother; for, while the postcards represent fingers holding toilet tissue, they must also represent verbal messages. Her bottom has been cleaned by insight!' (p. 95).

In these transition phases within the 'natural history' of the process, the working through that 'permits movement forward in the transference from one phase to another and finally to termination and self-analysis' depends on 'the content of the interpretations', not just the maintenance of the setting. It takes the form of demonstrating new equipment within the internal object, introjected from the external object:

> It is on the basis of an introjective identification with the newly equipped 'object' that the adult part of the personality improves its capacity for control over infantile structures and thus of

acting-out. This improved insight by way of introjective identification can be distinguished from mere intellectual insight.

([1967] 2018, p. 96)

The 'weaning' phase is dominated by fear of premature interpretation, interacting at infantile levels with the depressive concern for the 'babies', those imagined to be in future need. Even with young children, cooperation and interest in the work at this point can be 'astonishing'. A strong urge to self-analysis sets in and contrasts with the earlier pseudo-self-analytic attempts that were driven by envy and competitiveness. The analyst is now seen as presiding over the process in a way that sets an example for the patient to help them eventually assume these responsibilities. Above all, what regularly emerges is an experience of the beauty of the process. Dream life commonly takes the form of the patient watching a film or events but not being involved; or being engaged with others who are recognised as parts of himself. The realities of separation and introjection are flooded with the aesthetic impact of Bion's LHK (love, hate, knowledge), the aesthetic conflict.

Throughout the process, Meltzer emphasises that analytic work can only take place with the cooperation of the most adult part of the personality. This has nothing to do with age; it refers to the part which is best capable of introjective identification with internal objects:

> And so, to a greater or lesser degree, there is always in existence, if not always available for contact, a most-mature level of the mind, which, because of its introjective identification with adult internal objects, may reasonably be termed the 'adult part'. It is this part of the personality with which an alliance is sought and fostered during analytical work.
>
> ([1967] 2018, p. xix)

The hope of the analyst is that this 'adult part' will gain increasing control over the 'organ of consciousness', and thus of behaviour, not only for the purpose of increasing cooperation but eventually for the development of a capacity for self-analysis.

Ultimately the patient, like the analyst, will develop the special observational capacity that comes from directing the 'organ of consciousness' both inwards and outwards. Only when this self-analytic capacity has been sufficiently established within the patient can the transference relationship be relinquished and, potentially, an external friendship be established between analyst and patient. Meltzer said that the emergence of genuine gratitude was a sign that the analysis was finished. He wrote of a 'certain shyness about speaking of love in the transference and countertransference, for fear of appearing sentimental or of colluding in the covert aggression of the erotic transference' (Meltzer & Williams [1988] 2018, p. 25). The erotic transference is based on projection and control, and he warns that both analyst and patient 'tend to resist its dismantling'. Whereas the love that is earned during analysis is a 'conversation between internal objects', as in other life situations.

Perhaps inevitably, the process is not always taken through to its natural ending, weaning, but may be interrupted prematurely, or reach an impasse, and Meltzer discusses both situations in *The Psychoanalytic Process* and elsewhere. Yet when it does end, following the 'weaning' analogy, Meltzer (unlike many analysts) was happy to continue to supervise an ex-analysand's self-analysis, in particular by means of dream interpretation; and did not consider this at all incompatible with a friendship that could then continue outside the sphere of the transference.

Note

1 Meltzer is the patient with the dream about the boy, the snake, the girl and the lioness in Klein's (1963) paper 'On the sense of loneliness'. He called his analysis with her 'a wild ride'.

Key texts

Meltzer, D. ([1967] 2018). *The Psychoanalytical Process*. London: Harris Meltzer Trust.

Meltzer, D. ([1986] 2018). *Studies in Extended Metapsychology*. London: Harris Meltzer Trust.

Chapter 8
Transference and countertransference

As mentioned earlier, Meltzer regarded Freud's discovery of the transference as, together with Anna O's 'talking cure', the birth of the psychoanalytic method. This in itself took Freud by surprise, and he accepted the challenge, as in Meltzer's fable of the Emperor Freud's new clothes (see above in Part I). Like all scientific discoveries, the discovery of the naked reality of the transference was not the end of the story but the beginning of a logical, perhaps never-ending, evolution in which model and method were intertwined. Those who see psychoanalysis as an art-science will give credit to the value of immersion in a story, in order to allow the truth to 'slip through', as Bion put it: in particular the truth of not being in omnipotent control of one's own mind. The mind's gods are its internal objects and they lead development forwards while the self follows after; and this applies to the analyst as much as the patient. Following the account of a patient's dream of throwing lighted matches into the mouth of 'himself or another representation of himself', Meltzer concludes:

> This seems to me the role of the analyst—to strike fire in the mind of his patient. It is something that we would all feel fundamentally incapable of doing. We can't even carry on an interesting dinner table conversation, to say nothing of striking

fire into people's minds. No, if it weren't for the transference we would be absolutely helpless to assist our patients. It's the transference from these internal objects which enables us to seem to perform functions for the patient that are essential to the development of their thinking.

([1997] 2021, p. 114)

The analyst needs to beware of the illusion on the part of either himself or the patient that he knows the truth:

> The nature of transference, whether of a child, an adult or a patient, leads the patient to be convinced that the analyst knows the truth. Naturally the analyst does not know the truth and must attempt to stabilise the transference situation without feeling too overwhelmed. The great danger the analyst may encounter during his work is to begin to think he knows the truth. In analysis, for example, when the patient makes a step forward towards digesting a new idea, the analyst can see through his behaviour that a new idea is present, but cannot know what it is until it is described in his dreams. We find ourselves always in a situation of uncertainty.
>
> (2005c, p. 178)

Meltzer gives very limited value to the patient's history and says that the traditional view of using the transference to elucidate the history should really be the other way around:

> Always the movement should be in the anti-clockwise direction – the construction of the transference should be used for interpreting the meaning of the so-called facts of the history. I regard this re-constructing of the 'mythology' of the person's development as a product, and not a root, of the therapeutic impact of the psychoanalytical process.
>
> ([1984] 2018, p. 162)

The main analytic work, he said, was conducted in relation to the maternal transference, suggesting that because of this, one problem more common in men than in women analysts was that 'they feel as if the transference is to themselves and not to their objects':

> If they would step aside and allow themselves to function simply as presiding over and commenting as commentators on an interaction between the patient and their internal objects, they would not feel that restraint and they would not feel that embarrassment.
>
> ([1989] 2021, p. 31)

Analysis is not about the analyst's personal qualities but about their transference robes – a religious role. Analysts can gain relief from their own narcissistic identifications by recognising that they are merely the instrument of the process and its phantasy set-up, like a play, in the service of internal objects. Indeed, when asked towards the end of his life if he had practised psychoanalysis his own way (as in the Sinatra song, which he hated), he insisted: 'No, I've been done *its* way!' Psychoanalysis was itself an internalised aesthetic object, leading him and the others in the field onwards along logical lines – hence his adoption of the Bionic view of 'psychoanalysis as a thing-in-itself'.

The preformed transference

Much has been said about the notion of a false self (or similar denomination), but Meltzer pointed out as early as in *The Psychoanalytical Process* (1967) that there is also such a thing as a false transference. It could be quite easy for the analyst to be seduced by the patient or by themselves into the belief that what was taking place was a psychoanalysis when it was only a pretence. Bion too talks about a procedure that is 'just like' an analysis. At its extreme this would be what is known as 'folie à deux'. More 'normally' however – he suggests almost ubiquitously – there is a 'preformed transference' that has to be overcome and discarded before the real emotional transference reveals itself:

> It becomes clear that instead of this effortless attracting to the analytic setting all of the transference processes of the patient's life, it seems necessary to dismantle something that I've come to think of as the 'preformed transference' of the adult patient. The preformed transference, based on greater or lesser knowledge of or fantasies about the analytic method and the analytic experience, has to be taken down like an old shed at the bottom of the garden before anything new can be constructed. It can occur very quickly, in a few weeks, or it can take months or years to dismantle this preformed transference, a component of which is sometimes the erotic transference whose dismantling both analyst and patient tend to resist.
>
> (2000b, p. 2)

In particular, the preformed transference consisted in the patient's efforts 'to follow Freud's expectations regarding repetition compulsions' and to see themselves as repeating or bringing up the past. This 'endless repetition ... gives the appearance of being an analytical process and yet is not' ([2000a] 2021, p. 111).

The sign that it is the preformed transference, rather than the true transference, that is in operation, is the absence of surprise:

> Nothing surprises the patient – nothing the patient dreams, nothing the analyst says, comes as a surprise; and that of course is very discouraging to both patient and analyst. Whatever you say the patient's reply is always 'Oh yes, I have always known that.' One wonders, is it true? Well in a certain sense of course it is true. What we have to say is a thing that the patient has known as it were for millions of years. But the fact that they are not surprised that another human being should recognise this thing and be able to frame it in some sort of verbal or metaverbal vehicle of communication,

is evidence that some very powerful omniscience is being invoked by the patient.

([2000a] 2021, p. 111)

Indeed Meltzer always stresses that the patient knows himself intimately in a way that the analyst can never do; but his point is that this bored or irritable 'yes I know' is not true self-knowledge but a way of fending off a live transference relationship that could symbolise the present emotional situation.

It was Klein, he said, who in her 1946 paper on projective identification actually changed the concept of transference, although she did not claim to have done so. Working with children enabled her to see that analysis was not about repetition of the past but about externalising the current internal situation (relationships and identification processes) on to the analyst:

> While in Freud's hands, transference was an expression of the repetition compulsion and a repetition of past events in the transference situation to the analyst; Mrs Klein transformed this into a concept of the externalization of the internal situation onto the analyst, which therefore had an immediate implication. That is, the transference expressed in itself the patient's unconscious state of mind as represented by his infantile relationships to his internal objects and the identification processes that arose out of them. And that this is what was transferred into the outside world onto the analyst and manifest in the phenomenology of the consulting room.
>
> (1979, p. 8)

This altered view of the transference 'opened analysts' eyes to phenomena they hadn't previously looked at; and it brought in its wake this new interest in the countertransference as a tool, not just a nuisance'. It also enabled a differentiation between the analyst as an object of phantasy, and as an object of projection.

In order to make contact with the true infantile transference it is necessary to 'seek for the lost child' of the personality, which lights up the analyst's patience, tolerance, 'the music of his voice, the look in his eye' ([1992] 2018, p. 100). This is a much more active process with adults than with children, since as he explains in *The Psychoanalytical Process* (based primarily on work with children), the preformed transference is not a problem with children. Rather, it occurs with adults who, almost inevitably, have done a lot of reading about psychoanalysis, are well acquainted and interested in psychoanalytic theories and believe they understand the method. This 'knowing about' psychoanalysis then interferes with 'knowing', as in Bion's distinction between academic external information and internal learning from experience.

Observation and the countertransference dream

'Countertransference is everything in psychoanalysis', said Meltzer, and probably most would agree with this modern view:

> The historical idea that you must not communicate the countertransference is an illusion. You are communicating it in the music of your voice all the time. And you have to be a little bit careful about your music, so that it doesn't become tyrannical, or too pedagogical, and so on. But there is no way of hiding the countertransference. You can only modulate it to avoid excesses. It is absolutely what the patient hears: he hears the countertransference.
>
> (in Oelsner & Oelsner [2005], p. 458)

The analyst offers not only interpretation of content but an example of their thinking process, which can then be assimilated or introjected by the patient in their own way, as an internal function matched up with existing object relations. It is inevitably idiosyncratic and personal, and the introjected form will be likewise idiosyncratic. This is where the meaning lies – in the 'music' (discussed below).

Problems in the countertransference derive from the analyst being an object of projection by the patient (rather than an object of phantasy):

> It's necessary to receive that [projected] state of mind, but at the same time to recover from being dominated by it before you act in the countertransference. And I think, if the truth be said, that one always recovers a *bit* too late. Almost always, there's a note of anger in your voice, or an amorous note in your voice before you — but still, you recover before much damage is done. But I think the truth is that we do act in the countertransference, a little bit, very frequently, because it's very difficult to recover before you've been impelled into action to some extent.
> (1979, pp. 15–16)

Countertransference action is the opposite of what Meltzer calls the 'countertransference dream', his equivalent of Bion's 'reverie'. This is true 'analytical activity, namely a search for the truth', and the job of the analyst is to 'preside over the setting in a way which permits the evolution of the patient's transference'. The psychoanalytic discourse is largely 'of the patient's creation, through the symbol formation contained in his dream structures', although the analyst may 'introduce a certain amount of his own poetry – his own symbol formation' (in Williams [2010], p. 124). This however is not the same as the continuous countertransference dream which is a private response.

Meltzer sees the countertransference dream as a special type of observation that is alert to aspects of meaning that are still incipient, shadowy:

> It is difficult to explain the technique of counterdreaming. It is not enough to fall asleep while the patient is talking.

It requires a process of working over the material, focusing and selecting interpretive configurations awaiting a state of satisfaction (rest). The state of observation is essentially a resting state. It is also a state of heightened vigilance. I compare it with waiting in the dark for the deer, grazing at night, seen by their flashing white tails. This nocturnal vigilance is on the alert for movement of the quarry, part-object minimal movements that with patience can be seen to form a pattern of incipient meaning 'cast before'. This catching of the incipient meaning cast before is a function of receptive imagination – open to the possible, unconcerned with probability. Being rich with suspense, it is necessarily fatiguing, and fraught with anxiety. It is a trial of strength – and faith – that gives substance to terms such as resistance or retreat. However, it is a poetry generator.

In short, the countertransference is an emotional experience that must be caught in your dreams. Now the patient must attend to the analyst to interpret. How does he know what he is talking about? He doesn't – he is 'counterdreaming'; he has, in fact, abandoned 'thinking' (science) for intuition (art, poetry): the verbal tradition of Homer.

(2005c, p. 182)

Meltzer now describes counterdreaming as a 'technique', falling under the heading of psychoanalysis as an art form, incorporating Bion's vision of how meaning finds its way into the containing conversation in the form of 'the shadow of the future cast before'. The analyst's only claim to any special qualification in the consulting room encounter is 'his capacity to deploy his "organ of consciousness" inward to comprehend his countertransference'. He undertakes to use consciousness for the purpose of thought, rather than action: to 'contain the infantile aspects of the mind and only to communicate *about* them' ([1967] 2018, p. xviii). The analyst is an observer, and what he discovers about the patient is based on observation, not histories or theories. But this special type of observation is directed outwards and inwards simultaneously. Bion speaks of 'reading the marks made on oneself'. The part-object minimal movements are captured by their reflection in the mind of the analyst.

The nature of the countertransference dream became poetically clearer and more precise over the years. Meltzer said he was not a natural writer, but 'I can tell a good story if a patient will dream it for me' ([2002a] 2021, p. 5). For him, dreams were the landmarks of a patient's narrative. One of the 'turning-point' dreams he cites is that of a patient who dreamed of a firefighter trying to link hands with a man on a swaying crane, and eventually succeeding, which Meltzer said intuitively reminded him of an old silent movie with Harold Lloyd hanging from the arm of a clock at the top of a tower. He said he himself felt 'rescued' by his countertransference response: 'The genius of dreaming had rescued me from the dangers of interpretation which had been based entirely on countertransference feeling, not on evidence' ([2001b] 2017, p. 215). Before that point, he had not been aware that the patient's trust had 'lapsed' and that in a previous therapy she had become seriously suicidal.

Dream interpretation

Since dreams are a presentational form, we need to receive its manifestations in a congruent way, through the language of communication rather than the jargon of explanatory diagnosis. For this reason Meltzer preferred to speak of 'dream exploration' rather than 'dream analysis'. His view was that the patient (or rather his unconscious) is the creative force and this may be borrowed to enrich and enhance the creativity of the analysis, helping it to progress to the point at which both partners are responding to it as an aesthetic object in itself. Dreams, he said, 'come to the rescue' of the analyst's own poverty of symbol-formation. They facilitate the evolution of a private language between the analyst and the analysand, based on a long-term narrative of the patient's dreamlife (called by Bion 'the language of achievement').

Meltzer gives a detailed description in *Dream Life* of his own method or habit in listening to dreams. He explains that he listens with eyes closed whilst picturing to himself the 'stage-setting' of the dream with its various actors, 'some clearly parts of the self, some clearly alienated as objects', and their 'story' (distinguished, after E. M. Forster, from 'plot'). This is the exploration phase:

> I feel certain that the exploration is the more important, the more artistic aspect of the work. The patient's growing identification with the analyst's exploratory method is a far more important basis for the gradual development of self-analytic capacity than any striving towards formulation.
> ([1984] 2018, p. 147)

In dream interpretation it is necessary to find a 'congruence' between the two minds engaged; the analyst 'strives to match the poetic diction' of the dream (Sharpe's literary phrase) – a special view of interpretation. Meltzer compares this phase to the opening moves in chess or bridge, 'and the tension does not assert itself until the vague outlines of the pattern of the game begin to emerge': 'I consider this as essentially aesthetic, something to do with appreciating the formal and compositional aspects of the dream as an event of theatrical proportion' (p. 149).

After the initial pleasing absorption however, uncertainties arise, with problems of correspondence between his own translation as listener, and the words of the narrator: 'these two sets of description – the patient's primary one and the analyst's secondary one – do not necessarily tally' and anxiety and unrest can arise whilst this correspondence is adjusted:

> The pleasant game of exploration now begins to yield place to growing unrest and distress in the analyst, and the atmosphere of the consulting room can become thick with anxious expectation and incipient disappointment. This is certainly a moment when Bion's 'Column 2' becomes very real; that is,

> the tendency to make statements that are known to be false in order to hide one's ignorance from oneself and the patient. I find that it is my custom – one could hardly call it 'technique' – to start talking, just reviewing the material, sorting out with the patient the text of the dream, the associations, the links with previous material, waiting for something to happen in my mind but holding the situation in a quiet state to give my mind space and time to work. Once interpretive notions begin to form and the confusion gives way to excitement, cooperative work with the patient commences again. But now it is a tense situation, anxiety and resistance are incipient, and the easeful time afforded by the patient's distancing is at an end.
>
> ([1984] 2018, p. 150)

Given that telling a dream is the 'easiest way for the patient to be truthful with the analyst', remembering dreams may be resisted, but this is not to any specific insight but rather to the working relationship and the cooperativeness required. In the modern 'process' view of psychoanalysis, the term 'resistance' has come to mean 'resistance to deepening emotional involvement in the transference–countertransference process'. It applies to both patient and analyst. Meltzer does not see this as a feature of acting-in-the-transference but rather as driven by 'the intense intimacy of dream-analysis'. In accordance with the concept of aesthetic conflict, the emotional impact of imminent catastrophic change arouses fear and turbulence, in both parties. For 'no material that a patient brings to his analyst is as powerfully evocative as his dream material'. An analyst may forget many facts about his patient's life 'but he is unlikely completely to forget his patient's dream unless his resistance has prevented him from analysing it' (p. 179). He concludes:

> In my experience the emotional situation between analyst and patient at the non-transference level (as two adult people working together at a task with knowledge, skill and an agreed

format of procedure) at no point reaches such heights of pleasure, intimacy and mutual confidence as in the unique process of dream-analysis. The reason for this is to be found in the aesthetic level of experience in both participants which abandonment to the 'poetic diction' of dreams facilitates; it brings out artistic creativity in both partners and produces an oeuvre, the dream and its interpretation, which both members can experience as generated by combined creativity.

([1984] 2018, p. 182)

The interpretive phase of 'formulation' of the dream is accompanied by 'a sense of being in the presence of an aesthetic object' (p. 150). It is not one-step but builds up into a 'fabric of interpretation' via a spiralling movement, and may well not take place in a single session 'for a rich dream is constantly being retrospectively lit up in one aspect or another' in subsequent sessions. Nonetheless, Meltzer feels that the earlier phase of dream exploration is more satisfying for the analyst. In the translation from a visual to a verbal language, something is lost, and unless the analyst has a poetic capacity of their own, or an inspired 'lyrical moment', the dream's poetic diction is liable to be 'reduced to the prose of psycho-analese'. Meltzer did not however believe in staying silent, if a satisfactory interpretation failed to come up, as silence can be felt as persecutory. He said part of the purpose of speaking was to maintain a sense of communication. The analyst is probably better to concentrate simply on finding an interpretation that 'covers the material' and that may be considered as just a holding point – 'not *the* correct formulation, only *a* correct formulation' (p. 153).

A dream sequence to illustrate misconception

The following example of Meltzer's dream-work is a marriage between the analysis of a patient's dream sequence and Money-Kyrle's concept of 'misconception' – formulated in the 'brilliant paper' (Money-Kyrle 1968) which was at the time lying in the back of Meltzer's mind awaiting a realisation in the consulting room. As such it is also a demonstration of his view that advances in theory can promote new observations.

Although the idea of mismatch between mother and baby is familiar, dream evidence for it is not. Meltzer says this material represents 'the dimension of "relative speed" of mental functioning and behaviour between mother and baby (analyst and analysand)'. The patient had a series of dreams beginning with the key image of a corkscrew, or rather, a screw-cork where a wine-bottle had 'a corkscrew emerging from the cork as if the bottle were the handle of the corkscrew'; followed by a dream about two ways to cross a river with his fiancée – either passing the pornography shop (where there was 'no bridge') or the 'long way round, upstream' ([1981] 2014, p. 243). In the next dream the patient was behaving aggressively as chair of a meeting at his house which seemed to be named 'Dugger Austeads' (aus = out (in German); dug = nipple, as in Shakespeare's Juliet's weaning by the Nurse putting 'wormwood on her dugs'; Douglas referring to a past attempted homosexual seduction). In addition to the ordinary Kleinian interpretations possible (projective identification in the screw-cork etc.), Meltzer asks,

> Why is it implied that the weaning is brought about by some factor that spoils the baby's pleasure, by something wooden and worm-like penetrating his mouth? ... Does a concept of a primal misconception of the nipple help us to describe this enigma?
>
> ([1981] 2014, p. 246)

For the patient, nearing the weaning stage of analysis, seemed 'unable to enjoy his happiness'. Forthcoming marriage and the end of analysis were across the river, yet he could not find the route upstream and could no longer make an aggressive bee-line to his goal as in the days when he felt he was a better-daddy-than-daddy to both his mother and his sister who, like all the children, he felt was rather over-indulged by a mother too anxious to please them:

> Does a baby who is offered the breast when he is not yet hungry enough to be quite desperate for it quite naturally form the misconception that the nipple has come to open his mouth so that gurgles and saliva may issue forth for mummy's delight ... And does a baby with an over solicitous-for-his-happiness mother take this all too seriously, not seeing the joke?
>
> ([1981] 2014, p. 248)

Following this, the patient dreamed of two carriages, one dark and one white, which suggested his two ways of 'remembering' (i.e. his relation to the breast): factual diary-keeping *versus* creative living memory. The analyst felt a misconception had come to light as it was beginning to be rectified, and the four dreams came together in a single narrative, imagined from the patient's point of view:

> All my life I had thought that my mouth was a fountainhead of goodness and wisdom which people, starting with my mother, were constantly seeking to open by various devices, and that I could not refuse them. Resentment of this plundering of my mind made it necessary, I thought, to keep my memories carefully dismantled and stored away, while at the same time making me very cautious towards people who took any special interest in me. But now I am beginning to see that I have perhaps been the recipient of charity and that a precious object that can itself carry my memories, thoughts, and ideas has been bestowed upon me at very little cost to myself. Perhaps I jumped to a wrong conclusion years ago and did not realise what a long way round it would be before I would be able to bestow in charity a like precious object to anyone.
>
> ([1981] 2014, p. 250)

Finally, the story of the screw-cork concludes in a waking dream-image that flashes through the patient's mind while another dream is being analysed about the confusion between recipient and donor:

> He had experienced seeing a corkscrew 'worming' its way through the glass of the consulting-room window in front of him, moving forward in the plane of the window pane without shattering or cracking the glass, as it would do in the yielding material of a cork.
>
> ([1981] 2014, p. 250)

Meltzer finds this image could represent the process of rectifying the original misconception:

> his baby-tongue (the worm, as distinct from the wormwood nipple) slowly progressing in its clarity of understanding (the window) despite the pain (pane), drawing the interpretative milk from this talkative analyst.
>
> ([1981] 2014, p. 250)

In conclusion, he suggests that Money-Kyrle's concept of misconception adds a new dimension to existing ways of seeing developmental processes, making visible the complex interaction of mother and baby with special reference to 'fit' or 'congruence in mental functioning' in relation to matters such as temperature, distance and speed, all of which are relevant to the process of finding adequate realisations for innate preconceptions. While a 'misfit' between mother and baby, and likewise between analyst and patient, is 'conducive to a primal misconception of the relation of nipple to mouth, and thereby of interpretation to a patient's material', the deeply humanist view of Money-Kyrle has, Meltzer suggests, a much wider application, opening the way for investigating 'factors of innocent misunderstanding between people based upon discontinuity in their conceptual frame of reference, the "O" of their mental analytic geometry'. The analysis of a type of innocent or unintentional confusion, distinct from aggressive projection, adds a new dimension to Bion's work on disturbances of thought processes. It was Money-Kyrle's view (seconded by Meltzer) – not the expression of a 'sanguine disposition' but the result of 'experience of life, in peace and war' – that in such ways psychoanalysis, along with the arts and social sciences, could help elucidate disharmony between people on both personal and social levels, and enable them to live in peace and amity.

The clearing of misconceptions can thus be added to emergence from the Claustrum, and applies to both patient and analyst – a restoration of reality that reveals the positive qualities of the depressive position, so often obscured by its unfortunate denomination that suggests misery and depression:

> Either one is in a state of denial of psychic reality, ready to assume that common sense is adequate, that things are just what they seem, or one lives inside an object and naturally sees the world as a vale of tears and prison-house; or one lives in a family atmosphere dependent on the bounty and mystery of the natural world, which one may use, abuse or neglect. The only 'faith' that is required is an absolute belief in one's feebleness, ignorance, impotence and mortality, to open to view the beauty-of-the-world and passionate feelings.
>
> ([1992] 2018, p. 111)

Key texts

Meltzer, D. ([1981] 2014). Does Money-Kyrle's concept of misconception have any unique descriptive power? Reprinted in: Money-Kyrle, R. (2014). *Man's Picture of his World*, pp. 239–256. London: Harris Meltzer Trust.

Meltzer, D. ([1984] 2018). *Dream Life*. London: Harris Meltzer Trust.

Meltzer, D. (2005c). Creativity and the countertransference. In: Williams, M. H. (Ed.), *The Vale of Soulmaking*, pp. 175–182. London: Karnac.

Chapter 9
Technique

Meltzer says that supervisees always want to know about technique as if this were teachable in the sense of formal instruction. Yet he said that long experience of teaching helped him to notice things about his own clinical work that would otherwise have 'escaped attention', and that this was even more true of technique than it was of comprehending the content of the session. On the one hand, as he said in an interview on the subject of supervision, 'The rationale of technique is really just the rationale of human communication' which requires 'tact, delicacy and clarity' and 'that's all there is to it' (in Oelsner & Oelsner [2005], p. 459). On the other hand, he was well aware that this rationale is not so easy to follow. As he wrote in an earlier paper on 'Temperature and distance': 'Our so-called teaching of technique is a peculiar and ill-defined area – a mixture of basic technical principles, of technical ingenuity within this basic method, of stylistic elements, and even of inconsequential idiosyncrasy' ([1976] 2021, p. 87). While there is no problem in setting out the basic technical principles of the psychoanalytic method, it is more difficult to guide the management of ineffable events from outside the actual analytic relationship. It is even difficult to understand them in the 'repose' phase (as Meltzer calls it) of subsequent reflection.

The sense of conviction comes when confirmed by the interdigitation of different vertices: resulting, as Bion and Meltzer both say, in an 'aesthetic' feeling of rightness. This does not derive from a marriage of insight and judgement, but from a matching of the beauty of the material to a congruent formulation. Together these take on 'an existence beyond' – becoming a thing 'apart from ourselves' – and make the psychoanalytic process an art form ([1992] 2018, p. 73).

Music and interpretative exploration

Meltzer writes that the basic technical principles he employs are 'derived from Freud and Klein, modified by my own view of the method as process'. In essence, the analyst's task is to create and supervise the setting, as described above. In this process however, '*interpretation proper* as a metapsychological statement (with genetic, dynamic, structural and economic aspects of the transference defined) can be distinguished from more *general interpretative exploration* of the patient's material, which is intended to facilitate its emergence' ([1976] 2021, p. 88). 'Interpretation proper' can be written down, remembered, published; it belongs to a formal linguistic notation – the lexical level of language. 'Interpretative exploration' however is less easy to describe outside the confines of the consulting room. This is on the lines of Susanne Langer's distinction between discursive and presentational forms – all art forms being 'presentational' in their import, even when their medium is words. The conclusion is not that the content of interpretations has no importance, but that 'the importance they have is mainly that they confirm for the patient that you really are listening and thinking', not whether they are right or wrong: 'Either they fit the material or they don't fit the material'. Of equal or greater importance is the 'music': 'I think the relationship between analyst and patient is contained not just in the words, but in the music as well' (in Oelsner & Oelsner [2005], p. 456).

Meltzer's aesthetic philosophy followed in the Cassirer–Langer tradition, frequently referred to in his writings. Music and interpretative exploration are functions belonging to psychoanalysis as an art form. Its scientific aspirations, Meltzer believed, would only be realised some time in the distant future, and should not be pre-empted. The problem is that psychoanalysis is a *private* art form. Symbols emerge, slip away, transform, in a continuing process, in the transference dialogue; they are not captured for the benefit of an audience. How is it possible to describe or even observe the functioning of interpretative exploration within the psychoanalytic setting? Especially given the nature of the 'private language' that gradually takes shape within a particular transference relationship but that is very difficult to 'publish' outside that relationship. According to Neil Maizels, 'Whilst this sort of reflective adhocracy is often present in supervisory moments, it had never been taken so fully seriously, on an equal footing with levels of anxiety and "correctness" in interpretative work' (in Williams [2010], p. 21).

In the 'Temperature and distance' paper Meltzer considers 'the limits of technical ingenuity within the bounds of fundamental method' with special focus on 'ingenuity of verbal expression'. By this he means non-verbal expression as well: the tone, distance and music that modulate the interpretative exploration. This is to be distinguished from stylistic elements that are features of the analyst's personality, apparently trivial, yet which may appear in the material the form of projective mimicry. 'Where does ingenuity end and acting-in-the-transference begin?' Meltzer asks. He suggests that Freud's original advice to adopt a 'blank screen' demeanour circumvented the problem, and in any case, acting can be hidden behind a blank screen. Like all prescriptive technical advice it relates only to behaviour, not its meaning. Rather, Meltzer suggests, a more flexible mode of tonal dialogue can be fostered that is able to reflect the varying parts of the personality that are in the foreground, the distance between these parts and the analytic voice, and the direction of communication.

What is needed is to 'control the atmosphere of communication' through temperature and distance, using an interplay of the lexical and metaphoric levels of language and finding the appropriate tone of voice to respond to the part of the personality. Just as the mind is not a unity, neither is the person: they have adult parts, infantile structures, tyrannical parts, male and female parts and other 'classes' to which the patient belongs. An awareness of splitting processes helps to distinguish between them, and whether communicatively or in an acting role, each with its own language or way of talking. As always, the analyst's task is first of all one of observation – in this case, to detect which part is speaking:

> We can by this means utilise rather different languages as a directional advice, each different from the other in vocabulary, imagery drawn from the patient's speech and dreams, levels of education, degrees of vulgarity or refinement, etc. In addition to this directional device for addressing different parts of the patient's personality at different times, we can also modify the distance by not addressing the part concerned in our formulation at all, but rather, talking about that part to another, or by ruminating aloud in the presence of the patient, leaving it to his choice to listen or ignore.
>
> ([1976] 2021, p. 90)

Reviewing with hindsight his own practice, Meltzer observes that he tends to modify the direction and object of his interpretations according to whether they may increase or diminish pain – assuming the pain is there (even if not yet 'known').

> In general, interpretations referable to persecutory anxiety are likely to diminish the pain, and those referable to depressive anxiety to increase the suffering at the moment. Therefore, I seem to be more likely to address an interpretation of persecutory anxiety directly to the part in pain, and more likely to talk to the adult part about a part that is suffering from depressive anxiety.
>
> ([1976] 2021, p. 93)

The question of direction (that is, towards which part) is 'handled linguistically', using a personal vocabulary based on the patient's own familiar modes of expression or cultural background – from vulgarity to sophistication. Talking to the adult part about itself relates to the goal of engaging cooperation in the task of psychoanalysis as a work group: 'I notice that when problems of co-operation are at issue, I seem to talk to the adult part about himself'. This flexible use of vocabulary and tone of address is thus intimately connected to the transference relationship, and the need to link up with the 'lost child' and preverbal modes of communication.

All this forms part of the 'music' of the transference, which is founded on the primal mother–baby relationship and begins in utero:

> I think that the music of the human language and human voice is very primal. It is the link between mother and baby while it is still in utero: the music of the mother comes through to the baby. I think that the deepening of the analytic transference is very dependent on this music and much less dependent on the intellectual insight that you can communicate by interpretation.
> (Oelsner & Oelsner [2005], p. 456)

Potentially the music of the speaking voice can be modulated through 'its entire range' from 'monotone to full operatic splendour' ([1976] 2021, p. 90). But the analytic session is not an opera; it has to find its own analogies to this musical spectrum, controlling the 'atmosphere of communication' through temperature and distance. The same musical elements would be involved – tone, rhythm, key, volume and timbre (including, of course, silence) – but not on an operatic level.

> By modulating these musical elements, we can control the emotionality of the voice and thus what I mean by the temperature of our communication. This, in turn, has an impact on the

emotional atmosphere of the consulting-room and the reverberation between patient and analyst, variously heightening or damping this atmosphere.

([1976] 2021, p. 90)

The music is not detachable from the underlying identifications that are playing out in the theatre of phantasy where meaning is generated.

Meltzer calls this management of music, direction and atmosphere the acquisition of 'virtuosity', something which builds up only with experience. But it has nothing to do with linguistic virtuosity as such – as might apply in respective ways to say a poet, a politician or a lecturer. Instead it has its own rhetoric created within the setting and based on dreams, phantasy and babytalk, probably not even comprehensible to anyone outside that particular couple. In this sense psychoanalysis is protected from voyeurism by the nature of its own art form. The 'language of achievement' (as Bion calls it) is not publishable; what is publishable is the analyst's own experience of the relationship – the countertransference.

Confidence in being able to practise psychoanalysis as an art form is the analyst's best defence against institutional demands for 'action'. Action is expressed not only in protocol but in a judgemental manner of interpretation (used as diagnosis), which Meltzer regards as the main cause of the 'negative therapeutic reaction'. Instead, interpretation needs to take the form of thinking aloud in the presence of the patient, or their internal objects, and this allows it to find a music of its own that goes right back to the prenatal and preverbal, sensuous origins of language.

Technical problems of the Claustrum

To return to the question first posed in *The Psychoanalytical Process*: how can the analyst avoid self-harm (that is internally, regardless of external influence or criticism)? For the analyst, as the object of infantile dependence, is by nature inviting and containing projective identifications; these are experienced as countertransference which can contain and 'forestall the intrusive intention to some degree in the presence of the object' but less reliably during separations ([1992] 2018, p. 68), thereby increasing the pressure on the countertransference. However some technical problems may be soluble in terms of shifts in the analyst's attitude to his task.

As the picture of the countertransference makes clear, any analytical process is as much about the analyst as about the patient. Meltzer saw the chambers of the Claustrum – the internal house of psychopathology – as a feature of everybody's mind; the degree of imprisonment to be measured by the type and fixity of intrusive projective identification. Meltzer said, scratch the surface and the madness appears. Conversely, he said, 'the door is always open', even to the most ensconced part of the personality: there is two-way traffic.

In this context he thought it was crucial for the analyst to be clear, and make clear to the patient, that he is not an inmate of the Claustrum but a visitor. He sees around the situation but he does not live there. One day perhaps the patient may simply follow him out of the door, discarding the clothing of 'lies' (as Bion expresses it). Key to this potential freedom is which part of the personality is in control of the 'organ of consciousness', that is, attention. Meltzer always valued this idea of Freud's and gained support here from Bion; for it became evident that the countertransference is not just for emotional containment but for thinking about the problem, using this observational facility. The task of the analyst is widened, laying a greater burden but also pinpointing a means of tackling this expanded view of a corrective developmental experience:

> It seems likely that in most psychotic areas of the mind incipient thought is stifled and produces a debris of proto-phenomena (Bion's alpha-function in reverse, the genesis of hallucination and delusions, psychosomatic phenomena, and basic assumption group mentality). Where this debris of nascent thought is evidenced it may at times be possible for

the therapist to gather up the fragments and reconstruct the thought that would have developed had it not been stillborn.

([1986] 2018, p. 2)

The Kleinian view of restoring the babies of the internal mother also means restoring damaged fragments of proto-thoughts and putting them into useful operation, reconstructing the baby that is the new idea. Not just content, but thought processes and the links that bound them, were the concern of the psychoanalytic method.

Meltzer said he was glad to find a way of abandoning the concept of the death instinct, and to discard the moralistic attitude to the patient that it promoted (2000b, p. 10). The attack on thinking and negative links described by Bion, as a result of his insight into group mentality, gives the analyst a more secure basis for facing up to perversity and avoiding the seduction that could creep in when the only conceptual tool was 'integration' of splitting processes:

> This avenue of enquiry into group communication processes is surely a Bionic addition to our equipment for investigating the workings of narcissism. Nowhere is it more clear than with perverse areas of the personality which so quietly drain the vitality of object relations. And here Bion's formulation of positive and negative emotional links sheds a brilliant light. 'But am I not a part of this man's emotional life?' the perverse area seems to say, claiming a certain respectability and rightful share in the world of human intimacy. A dualistic theory, of life and death, of creative and destructive drives, gives no definitive answer except a grudging, 'Yes, but you must be subservient, integrated for good and creative ends', something the perverse aspect will smilingly accept, secretly triumphant. But when the perverse trends are recognised as anti-emotions, minus L, H and K [love, hate and knowledge], no ground need be yielded to them in compromise.

([1986] 2018, p. 252)

The previous 'dualism' on which both Freudian and Kleinian psychoanalytic theory was based leaves the analyst vulnerable to perversity; but with Bion's distinction between positive and negative links, the uselessness of perversity becomes a 'drain on vitality' and can be confronted within the analysis.

The Bionic extension, says Meltzer, opened up 'the vast area of mindlessness in mental life' ([1978] 2018, vol. 3, p. 125) and changed the analyst's view of his task in the consulting room, whilst also bringing to light the corresponding danger to the analyst is of having his own thought processes shattered. He did not find Bion's Grid of direct use in the consulting room, but reflecting outside, it enabled greater skill in detecting equivocal and defensive language and their disguise of defective logic, 'pseudo-quantifications, false equations and spurious similes':

> Taken together these tools for minute scrutiny of processes of thought and communication place the analyst in a far stronger position than ever before in the struggle to wrest infantile structures from the domination or influence of destructive parts of the personality which organise the narcissistic or basic assumption groupings internally or in the outside world.
>
> ([1986] 2018, p. 252)

Bion's ideas about thinking versus mindlessness also helped to differentiate genuine technical problems from institutional requirements, based on mindless obedience to basic assumption groupings. Meltzer said that 'breach of technique' could be defined only by the analyst as an individual, not by external rules: the analyst must be clear about his own customary procedures, and the reason for them, in order to be flexible when this might help the patient, whilst able to distinguish any changes in routine from countertransference action. This could not be defined from the outside. He was savage about the 'poisoned atmosphere' of the 'corporate view' of psychoanalysis and felt that, ultimately, a moralistic adherence to basic assumptions and hierarchy (over and above daily convenience) would infect the intimate dialogue of the consulting room, and the analyst would himself become confused between K and minus K.

It is necessary to be vigilant and continually ask the question:

> How is one to distinguish phenomena in our patients and ourselves which are the consequences of emotional experiences which have been subjected to symbol formation, thought, judgment, decision, and possibly transformation into language, from others which are habitual, automatic, unintentional?
> ([1986] 2018, p. 12)

In Meltzer's vision, this difference between the mental and protomental, real thinking and non-thinking, became a core feature of psychoanalytic work, linking up with phenomena such as the preformed transference and taking over from the traditional Kleinian goal of integration of split-off parts. Instead, the task of the analyst is to 'perform the alpha function of which the patient is incapable' in a particular area of experience: This 'excursion into imaginative or dream-thought' was illuminated greatly by the work with autistic children, whose special type of imprisonment demanded that the analyst perform the role of 'speaking object' and invite them into three-dimensionality. Yet, as Meltzer always stresses, the autistic condition illuminates a facet of mental structure that is universal.

In terms of the Claustrum, Meltzer has some specific advice. The way is to make clear that the door is open, and the analyst is a visitor, with the restricted role of tour guide. It is necessary to avoid intimacy, not to collude with a false transference with its 'mutual seal of approval'. In the Claustrum the patient has no personality of their own, just adaptation to the claustrophobic world. There is 'no space' for a genuine infantile transference; the consulting room is 'just a cubicle in an institution' and the analyst is seen not as an individual but as 'a representative of a particular institution called psychoanalysis, with its hierarchy and its Kafkaesque mysteries'

([1992] 2018, p. 97). The governing fear is that of expulsion. Yet the only state in which there is no door is the 'nowhere' state of schizophrenia, the world not of projective identification of delusion, built from 'failed symbol formation – the debris of alpha-function in reverse' (p. 114). Meltzer says this state is basically inaccessible, and that he has never spoken to a part of the personality that was actually inside the delusional system: 'That is, I've heard them speak, but I've never been able to understand anything they were talking about. But I have talked to many parts of the personality teetering on the brink' (1979, p. 18).

It is only possible to work with parts of the personality that are not ensconced inside the object in a claustrophobic world. There is always some part of the personality living outside the object, which can be contacted and worked with if the analyst can persist in remaining outside. When, after a protracted struggle (by the analyst) the patient becomes truly aware that the analyst lives outside, there are dreams of coming out, encountering pain, hurrying back in, etc., and images of family life begin, as opposed to domination by values of respectability and survival. The dweller in the internal head–breast feels regret for wasted time; the genital-dweller feels dirty and enters the latency period; the rectum-dweller is left with a severe depressive problem owing to actual harm they may have done to others. The 'lost child' of the personality becomes visible. The patient throws off what Bion calls their 'exoskeleton':

> Once the patient does begin to emerge – although patients oscillate and run back in as soon as they can, because what they meet when they come out is rather terrible depression and a sense of wasted time in their lives, and 'it's too late for this' and 'too late for that', and so forth – things do settle down into an analysis that is really, by and large, a pleasure, because the patient becomes able to cooperate and becomes interested in the analytic work, and then it becomes cooperative work – and *that* is really where the pleasure lies, in the sense of cooperation.
> (2000b, p. 4)

Supervision as a dimension of clinical work

Meltzer had a particular interest in teaching and supervision. Much of the material in his later books derives from teaching situations, and this often 'marvellous' material (he said) constituted much of his pleasure in the work, especially in later years. He taught in many countries, either occasionally or regularly, and also kept up postal supervisions over long periods with both supervisees and ex-analysands. From the early 1970s he began to accompany his wife Martha Harris, who had taken over Esther Bick's infant observation seminars in Novara, and their teaching of child and adolescent analysis expanded throughout Europe and Scandinavia, especially in Italy (Novara, Rome and Perugia) and France (the GERPEN – *Groupe d'Etudes et de Recherches Psychoanalytiques pour le Développement de l'Enfant et du Nourisson*). They also taught in South America where Meltzer, also in the wake of Bick, began to visit in the 1960s. Meltzer also gave many talks and supervisions at the White Institute in New York and the Psychoanalytic Center of California. He believed that widespread teaching, crossing cultural and institutional barriers, was key to the survival of psychoanalysis as a creative force in the world.

Although he became a good speaker with an off-the-cuff virtuosity (he did not believe in writing down his talks – they were all transcribed afterwards) he saw the real teaching as taking place in supervision or small atelier sessions. In this context, he became interested in the nature of supervision and the relationship between supervisor and supervisee, which he saw as having certain essential parallels with that between analyst and analysand but less intense, more relaxed and more consistently a work group rather than a basic assumption group. And this could be extended to the way in which all participants in a seminar are helped to learn from experience, even if it is not directly their own. It is a special type of identification in which nobody can be a voyeur: an atmosphere in which competition and criticism are excluded and empathy and self-knowledge are promoted.

The dynamics of supervision are presented in various writings. In *Dream Life,* using the example of a seminar in which he and Harris comment in tandem on a case presented by a child psychotherapist, he suggests the seminar situation may be compared to the analyst listening to a patient's dream. The work with this particular young child was, like that with autistic children, 'non-verbal in its true sense' and embodied in action. It is an example of the kind of thinking that is not yet communicable in words, and this is the task of the seminar. When it arrives in the seminar, the child–therapist interaction is itself the dream, and the interventions made step by step as the material is recounted have the role of interpreting the *interaction* (not solely the child or the therapist). In 'sharing the experience through imagination with the therapist' she is helped to discover 'not only the meaning of [the child's] behaviour but of her own as well', and this is the prime lesson for all the group:

> Of course it will be seen that the seminar 'analysts' do not in fact, any more than do analysts in their consulting rooms, confine themselves to the mere transformation of the visual image communicated by the therapist's account into verbal form in order to define the *meaning* of the scene; they also, on the basis of experience and conceptual framework, make comments which attempt to explore the *significance* of the interaction and the mental states they portray. This division between *transforming* the expression (the symbolic form) and *discerning* the significance of the meaning thus transformed, is in keeping with Freud's original description of his method (see 'The Dream of Irma's Injection') ... But here we have a more basic task of establishing that *the dreamer is the thinker* and the analyst is *the comprehender of his thought.* By communicating his dream in whatever symbolic form is most available to him, action, play, pictorial or verbal – perhaps a capable musician might do it musically – the dreamer enlists the aid of the analyst to transform the evocative descriptive language into the verbal language of the description of meaning, the first

move towards abstraction and sophistication. By this means the thoughts are placed in a form where *thinking* in Bion's sense can commence, that is the manipulation of thoughts by processes of reason. This latter would include thinking about the processes of thought itself – thinking about thinking.

([1984] 2018, pp. 52–53)

Atmosphere is all-important, and the seminar leaders, Meltzer and Harris, on the basis of 'experience and conceptual framework', constitute a type of combined object in relation to the 'dream' of the seminar-as-container. This dream derives from the dream-encounter between child and therapist which has already been transformed into a form of thinking, and it now undergoes a further level of abstraction, available to all the seminar participants, in the process of being digested.

In an interview conducted in 1999 by Mirta and Robert Oelsner (2005) Meltzer emphasises that, as with the analyst in the consulting room, he, the music and the atmosphere are the most important elements, as they are within the psychoanalytic setting. It is the supervisor's job to make sure the atmosphere is so unthreatening that they can bring 'honest material', rather than to make a case for their interpretations. This was not only because he saw interpretation as secondary, but because evaluating its correctness or otherwise tended to give the impression of sitting in judgement: 'young people are very shy about their interpretations and feel threatened the moment they tell them to you'. And from the supervisor's point of view, it prevents the full imaginative immersion in the material that is necessary for identification. Instead it is better to 'sweeten the music a bit with your own music', through an attitude of kindness and humour that then percolates through all the layers – supervisor, analyst and patient.

For the supervisor also has a countertransference experience of the patient, at one remove, mediated by the analyst. As the analyst's thinking process sets an example to the patient, so it does to the supervisee. Meltzer, like Bion, points out that nobody can ever know the patient as well as they do themselves. It is thus important for the supervisor to demonstrate their capacity not to interpret in a judgemental manner – this is what the 'wisdom' of the more experienced person consists in:

> Older analysts certainly have had experience of many more clinical situations and therefore are expected to have, and do have, richer powers of discriminating between one analytic situation and another; and this they contribute, or should contribute. It is very much in the spirit of psychoanalysis that this is meant to be a feeding situation – and not force feeding, but a feeding situation in which what you have to offer is laid before the student or the supervisee for him to select what suits him.
> (in Oelsner & Oelsner [2005], p. 455)

This does not mean the supervisor should not put forward his ideas, but that they should be offered like food and 'made palatable', in the hope that the analyst's home cooking can be digested:

> I think it must be left really to the richness and the power of your ideas about the clinical material to make it palatable to the person who is being supervised, and you must try to avoid any kind of imposition of your ideas.

The best way to do this, he reiterates, is to 'stick to the clinical material, and not to wander into theoretical situations'. The supervisor has the opportunity to 'leaven' the analyst's entrenchment in theory and to 'lighten and loosen' obsessionality so that things can start moving. It is what happens with the patient that counts.

When asked if he ever commented on his opinion of the supervisee's countertransference, he pointed out emphatically that the only place for that was in his personal analysis. The supervisor can be concerned only with their own countertransference identification: 'My job as supervisor is to participate in the countertransference and to give voice to it in the music and words of interpretation, but not to comment on the analyst's countertransference because that is really none of my business'. Supervision is thus not like a master class in music but 'more of a participation – more like playing in the orchestra, just contributing'.

Meltzer's ultimate words of advice to future psychoanalysts were simply: 'Good luck'. As he ended one of his last public talks in 2002 at a conference organised by the Psychoanalytic Group of Barcelona:

> Well that's it. The enemy is retreating – not from your wisdom but from their folly, from their having attempted to capture a frozen space and getting themselves frozen in the process. That's the kind of game you've been playing. Now the survival in this kind of game depends on what is called good luck. Good luck. And when you translate 'good luck', it means, trust in your good objects. Good luck for the survival that you never could have planned, and that happened in spite of all your cleverness and ingenuity.
>
> ([2002b] 2021, p. 172)

Key texts

Meltzer, D. ([1976] 2021). Temperature and distance as technical dimensions of interpretation. In: Williams, M. H. (Ed.), *Selected Papers of Donald Meltzer*, vol. 3, pp. 87–98. London: Harris Meltzer Trust.

Meltzer, D. ([1992] 2018). *The Claustrum*. London: Harris Meltzer Trust.

Oelsner, M., & Oelsner, R. (2005). About supervision: an interview with Donald Meltzer. *British Journal of Psychotherapy,* 21(3): 455–461.

Chapter 10
Beyond the consulting room

Just as within psychoanalysis, the sense of conviction or truth occurs when the beauty of the material is added to the matching formulation, and individuals seek for 'congruence' in their internal object relations, so is it in terms of making a creative link with other disciplines or modes of working. A match or congruence is required, not a domination of one discipline by another, so that something new can be created, or rather, create itself.

For Meltzer, the most important areas of work were: intimate personal relationships, such as family life; and – in the outside world – artistic-scientific, and educational. These were areas in which valency was available to link up creatively with psychoanalysis. Within the evolution of his own method and model, closeness to infant observation and child education (working with Bick and Harris) was interwoven with Bion's speculations about prenatal life and personality groupings and with artists' imaginative depictions of creative versus claustrophobic inner space.

These creative links are embodiments of psychoanalysis as a 'thing-in-itself', the Kantian phrase that Meltzer adopts from Bion: implying an essence that takes on substance by means of work, both inside and outside the consulting room.

Psychoanalysis as a thing-in-itself

Meltzer saw the individual analyst as developing in tandem with psychoanalysis as a spiritual phenomenon (not as a political movement). The real psychoanalytic movement is not a political entity, though it is a global one. Development takes place by making emotional, cognitive and spiritual links with other fields, other people, just as (within the individual) other parts of the self. It is important that these links are of the Bionic type – that is, mutual, not colonising or explanatory. As a result of work in the consulting room – a private space with wider implications – something new could be born. It emerges from the conjunction between two fields or vertices that have discovered 'congruence in form and function' – the definition of a true symbol ([1984] 2018, p. 81).

Meltzer always believed, or hoped, that psychoanalysis could be a revolutionary force from society's inside, not simply an uneconomic mode of therapy for a small number of individuals. His interpretation of Bion (who was of very different political orientation) focuses on the impact of 'catastrophic change' whether in the mind or society; the 'thing-in-itself', once it has lodged in an existing structure, pulls it forward in line with its godlike/noumenal origins (Bion's 'alignment with O'):

> Taking the religious vertex Bion shows us a view of psychoanalysis that is of this sort: that great ideas exist in the world, that they are discovered by thinkers and transmitted for use to non-thinkers, for which purpose they must find a 'language', not necessarily verbal, that can both contain the idea without being exploded by its pressure of meaning nor be so rigid as to compress the idea and thus reduce its meaningfulness.
> ([1978] 2018, vol. 3, p. 111)

Meltzer, as we see, regards Bion's conception of the pre-existing idea of psychoanalysis as a feature of the 'religious vertex'. The religious vertex has nothing to do with institutionalised religion, any more than psychoanalysis can be defined by psychoanalytic institutions. It is one of Bion's three core cognitive vertices – art, science and religion – and for Meltzer it followed rationally from Klein's 'theological' model in which development takes place under the aegis of internal objects. Meltzer was among those who see the psychoanalyst as an artist-scientist. The mind is engaged in a 'discovery' mode rather than one of 'invention', seen in terms of a Platonic system:

> [Bion] wishes to treat 'psycho-analysis' as a thing-in-itself which existed in the world prior to its discovery by the mystic genius of Freud (big or little does not matter) who gave it form in his writing and practice and teaching.
> ([1978] 2018, vol. 3, p. 111)

The thing-in-itself relates to the idea of immanence in transcendence, an 'existence beyond oneself', as Emily Bronte's Catherine put it in *Wuthering Heights*. Not however an existence which has left the world behind, but one which has revealed a new dimension beyond the conjunction or coincidence that brought it into view. In Bion's terms it is caught in a conjunction of vertices, or an intersection with O.

The idea, with its origins in O (origin or object), is mediated by internal objects into visible human form, taking shape in 'a "language", not necessarily verbal' – a concept very familiar to poets and artists. Psychoanalysis is one of those languages. This is what Meltzer means by calling psychoanalysis an art form, over and above technical matters. The psychoanalytic consulting room is, he said, 'a forcing house for symbol formation'. Although the material is not really in publishable form (unlike art symbols) the process has wider ramifications. The underlying idea or 'underlying pattern' (Bion) penetrates the human mind and lodges there in a very local and specific way; it becomes manifest. The process is called thinking.

Discovering an idea, or giving birth to a preconception, a latent 'thing-in-itself', brings a 'catastrophic change' to the existing situation. This may be a large idea, such as the idea of psychoanalysis, or it may be a small intimate idea as in a personal dream. The idea results in a new way not just of looking but of being, of experiencing reality, and the process of impact and absorption is equivalent, whatever the size and scale of the idea – whether it is small enough to be contained within an individual mind, or changes the structure of society:

> Words like 'messianic', 'god', 'establishment', 'explode', etc., carry what [Bion] would call the penumbra of bigness, importance. To understand him one must put this aside and think of little messiahs, little gods, little explosions as well. The question of size in cosmic terms is irrelevant. Quantity has really dropped away from his work. Everything is quality now, so it does not matter if it is psychoanalytical microbiology or psychoanalytical astronomy we think we are dealing with, the qualities are the same.
>
> ([1978] 2018, vol. 3, p. 110)

The catastrophic impact of the new idea, on a societal level, cannot be safely contained and therefore is invariably modified (which Meltzer always distinguishes from 'modulated'), either by watering it down until it appears respectable or by ousting it as heresy:

> From this arose, by virtue of this new thing being uncontainable by the medical establishment, a new messianic establishment, eventually the International Psychoanalytic Association, whose function was both evangelical and conservative.
>
> ([1978] 2018, vol. 3, p. 111)

The institutional level, in Bion's (1970) ecclesiastical model, deflects the vital impact of new ideas by enshrining the occasional genius as a messiah to be worshipped and ignored. As Martha Harris pointed out before Bion himself died and became popular:

> The dependent group structure so often manifests itself in the reliance upon a crystallised selection of the theories of Freud (the original Messiah), sometimes pitted against a similar extrapolation from Melanie Klein (a latter day saint). Bion is unlikely to escape the same fate.
> (Harris [1978] 2018, p. 31)

On the individual level, however, or within the 'work group of two' inside the 'forcing house' of the consulting room, as in the artist's studio, the idea may find containment and the pain aroused by its turbulence can be modulated, transformed and expressed. But it does not belong to either partner; it belongs to the relationship. The fitting of the analyst's attention to the patient's cooperation makes a container for the symbol of that emotional moment, and the symbol is created by the aesthetic object that is the psychoanalytic method. As Bion would say, this object has 'valency', the capacity to attach to other areas of human activity which are likewise polyvalent rather than closed off. It is where psychoanalysis meets the world.

Psychoanalysis and the arts

One of the main, now well-acknowledged, ways in which psychoanalytic ideas find a useful home in the world is through connections with the arts, probably the visual and literary arts in particular. Meltzer said he was introduced to classical art when he was taken by his parents on a grand tour of Italy aged eight, and ever after maintained his interest. Literature he discovered much later, recognising that 'through books one can discover one's identifications'; indeed, before delving into fiction, he found a 'spouse' for Melanie Klein in his mind in D'Arcy Thompson's *Growth and Form* which was his 'undergraduate Bible' ([2002a]

2021, p. 5). In addition to his serious study of the philosophy of language, his interest in aesthetics was developed, amongst other ways, through his relationship with Adrian Stokes, both within and outside the Imago Group, where the relevance of psychoanalysis to the wider culture was discussed during the 1950s and 60s. Following that, the Kleinian spatial geometry of the internal mother, as experienced in psychoanalysis, was linked in Meltzer's model with the parallel art form of literary criticism through the collaboration with Meg Harris Williams in *The Apprehension of Beauty* (1988), with its core principle of aesthetic conflict. Meltzer says, 'the application to literary criticism and the differentiation of true and false art found a new language in this spatial dimension' (Meltzer & Williams [1988] 2018, p. xxv). These links with the arts, in which the drama between object-dependency and narcissism finds realistic expression, often at the expense of the artist, helped to clarify and make vivid psychoanalytic conceptions of health *versus* pathology.

For Meltzer, art work is not sublimation (a defence) but one of the highest forms of work, that is, a service to humanity. Art criticism or aesthetics, as an art form in itself, has parallels with the psychoanalytic process not just in its content but in its form; and there is scope for mutual enrichment. He said that 'understanding of the structuring of dreams … may also feed back to aesthetics as an aid to investigate composition in the various fields of art, a huge undertaking richly begun by Adrian Stokes in his many publications' ([1984] 2018, p. 123). In both dreams and art forms, he explored formal qualities such as structure and composition, in addition to iconographic content. He felt this structural analogue between disciplines could be more fruitful than the restricted meanings achieved by interpretation, when one side trains its reductive viewpoint on the other. He writes of the search for 'congruence of internal objects' ([1984] 2018, p. 45) within a psychoanalysis or other intimate relationship, and something equivalent was his vision of a creative relationship between art forms: a relationship from which new symbolic forms may emerge. These are a feature of the three-dimensional rather than linear dimension, when psychoanalysis is considered as an art form in itself, rather than as an explanatory science.

In a discussion with Stokes 'Concerning the social basis of art', first published in 1963 and reprinted in *The Apprehension of Beauty*, Meltzer considers another aspect of psychoanalysis' relationship with the arts, namely the state of mind of the artist. He and Stokes consider the artist's creativity in its social context, and the nature of the anxiety or different types of anxiety that derive from the internal rhythm of attack-and-reparation – far greater than the anxiety of publication so often talked about:

> If we say that the artist performs acts of reparation through his creativity we must recognize that in the creative process itself, phases of attack and phases of reparation exist in some sort of rhythmical relationship. This implies that the artist, at any one moment of time in the creative process, finds his objects to be in a certain state of integration or fragmentation; he consequently experiences a relative state of integration or fragmentation within the infantile components of his ego in relation to his objects. It must be recognized that this process necessarily involves great anxiety.
> (Meltzer & Williams [1988] 2018, p. 222)

This means anxiety of both types – depressive and persecutory. The focus is on 'security' not 'safety'; art, like development, is by nature risky. 'The very heart of the depressive position is the realisation that security can only be achieved through responsibility'; it depends on the relation with internal objects.

Meltzer and Stokes stress the difficulty of the task, not the neurosis of the artist. Inevitably there are times when the artist projects 'excessively' (in the sense of attacks) the audience 'due to the complications of the guilt involved, or excessive in the sense of endangering the ongoing nature of his own dynamic process'. At the same time however, the artist's communication with the public is itself via projective identification, a necessary feature of art's social impulse. Consequently the public too are liable to feel confused in the face of new art, until the 'object' behind it becomes visible. It is for this reason – the hidden meaning – that Meltzer, in another paper, warns that the difference between art and pornography is never superficially evident; but that 'experience in the consulting room should enable us to derive indicators of a structural, rather than descriptive, sort, for our external judgement of works of art as objects – aesthetic objects' ([1973] 2018, p. 202).

Of those for whom art-viewing is 'an important part of their inner-life processes', the relationship formed with the mind of the artist, as embodied in the work, is far from play or entertainment, and much closer to the stresses of intimate relationships in general:

> I think that the viewer we have in mind is not at all at play: while his social relationship to his companions may be part of his play life, towards art he is *at work,* exposing himself to a situation of intensely primitive (oral) introjection through his eyes or ears or sense of touch. That is, he enters a gallery with the aim of carrying out an infantile introjection, with the hope, in its constructive aspects, of obtaining something in the nature of a reconstructed object. Conversely, in a masochistic sense, a viewer may be going to expose himself to the experience of having projected into him a very destroyed object or a very bad part of the self of the artist.
> (Meltzer & Williams [1988] 2018, p. 229)

Until the art work becomes known, the potential for the viewer's own self-destructive impulses exists and may be activated. Stokes relates the oral introjection performed by the viewer to the 'enveloping action of a work of art and to the breast relationship from which it derives', pointing out that he refers to the work's formal impact rather than its subject matter. This is why an ugly or horrific subject can still refer the viewer back to a 'good breast', a 'reconstructed whole-object' that can contain the disintegration of the infantile parts of the self.

The artist's ability to produce 'successful' works, in this special sense of ultimate containment, is (Meltzer believes) a product of gradual maturity 'not only of mastery over his materials but … of his relationship to his own primal good objects'. The motivation to produce such works derives from both the desire to be understood by others (an appreciative response) that encourages carrying on; but more importantly (from the point of view of social value) it comes from 'feelings of concern for "all the mother's babies"'. Art then becomes a 'sermon to siblings' which intends unconsciously to project both the restored object and the artist's own achieved capacity to bear depressive pain:

> Seen from the spectator's angle, the viewing, and the yearning to view, the work of masters would not only derive from the relationship to the product of art as representing the mother's body and the contents of her body; it also represents the relationship to the artist as an older sibling from whom this kind of encouragement and help in achieving a sufficient devotion and reverence for the parent is sought.
> (Meltzer & Williams [1988] 2018, p. 232)

Stokes confirms the idea of the artist as an older sibling with his own term 'brotherliness'. They both clarify that this social valuation does not mean an art work should contain sociological comment; the value is internal and can then be deployed outwards into society and other forms of activity and work. Socially of course, as Meltzer points out, the reverence that results from recognition of value applies to dead artists; for living siblings, there is more often neglect, dismissal or condemnation:

> To sum it up psychoanalytically, until they become 'masters' they are treated as new babies at the breast, by a world full of

siblings who, while deriving hope from the new baby's existence and performance, cannot control their envy and jealousy.
(Meltzer & Williams [1988] 2018, p. 238)

And this itself is referable to what he later formulates as 'aesthetic conflict', which often takes the form of beauty-in-ugliness, that is, the beauty has to be earned psychically by the viewer as it was earned by the artist, in a way that external nature cannot model: 'In nature we can find reflected the beauty we already contain. But art helps us to regain what we have lost'.

The child in the family in the community

Meltzer, as already noted, placed a special value on the intimate type of education called 'learning from experience', which he regarded as closely related to the practice of psychoanalysis. He saw the dissemination of ideas as a mysteriously transferential and identificatory process of inspiration, rather than of dogmatism. This capacity to receive ideas begins in childhood and is fostered by the family with its educational role; and here Meltzer is interested especially in the psychological ambience, rather than formal acquirements, which are a different function.

On one level, he saw family and school as both cooperating in the educational growth-cycle delineated by Alfred North Whitehead in terms of a rhythm of 'romance, precision, and generalisation', which Meltzer says has a psychological link to the nature of the oedipal conflict, latency structure and adolescent organisation ([1973] 2018, p. 196). Within this cycle, he saw educability in terms of Bion's distinction between protomental (unthinking) and mental (thinking) tendencies. This is a different matter from academic achievement. From early childhood the two levels of mental operation interplay and 'compete for the soul of the child'. Both are an inevitable part of living in the outside world, but the danger lies in the primitive protomental level becoming an 'exoskeleton' blocking the observation of emotional facts that could develop the mind.

It is this internal war of educational principles which can be greatly influenced by the family environment. But first, before any practical suggestions can be made, it is necessary to understand what types of family environment there are, in psychoanalytic terms. In 1976 he and his wife Martha Harris were asked by the Organisation for Economic Co-operation and Development (OECD: based in Paris) to produce a psychoanalytical model of 'The child in the family in the community'. Harris, originally trained as a teacher, conceived the educational programme for child psychotherapists at the Tavistock Clinic, on the basis of the principles 'enabling and inspiring': that is, Meltzer said, to 'discourage elitism, competitiveness and exhibitionism' and to 'minimise obedience and persecutory anxieties'.[1] These principles govern the 'learning from experience' that constitutes genuine education also in the family and community, as set out in the Model (whose text was written mainly by Meltzer). Seen psychologically, the underlying pattern of educational types goes beyond cultural differences:

> The structure of models of family life has deep roots in psychic reality, not in political and social values of the moment. Its universal character therefore permits hope that there could be international agreement based on these permanent values.
> (Meltzer & Harris [1976], 2013, p. 2)

In the Model, the family is taken as an educational institution, and like all such institutions or communities, the problem or task is how to engage with the child's own innate thrust for development. If there is mismatch or tyranny in the relationship between child and educator there is liable to be delinquency or conformity, rather than education; indeed, delinquency and conformity can be considered two sides of the same coin. It is the battle between truth and lies:

All the so-called mechanisms of defence are lies, known to be false but adopted as the basis of values, attitudes, judgements and actions in a manner essentially cynical ... In the unconscious their most primitive form is the acceptance of false symbols to represent the emotional situation; but more sophisticated forms of lying distort history (memory), introduce false logic, semantic ambiguities, spurious generalizations, counterfeit emotions.

(Meltzer & Harris [1976], 2013, p. 37)

Lies affect the individual's capacity to see truthfully not just the inner world but also the external world – something which had previously been left out of the psychoanalytic picture since it was assumed that the external world is somehow obvious and objective, seen by everybody in the same way. The new picture of learning processes emphasises that perception is not separable from endowing with meaning, and the capacity to observe all types of 'reality' is not automatic but depends on the links made between the child's innate qualities and their environment. The key categories of this educational picture were also summarised by Meltzer in *Studies in Extended Metapsychology* ([1986] 2018) in the chapter entitled 'Family patterns and cultural educability'.

In the Model five intimate ways are described: learning from experience, learning from projective identification, learning from adhesive identification, learning from scavenging and learning from delusion. 'All contrast with learning about'. In other words, all these five are personal modes that reflect a particular mental state or stage in development and its mental geography. These days they have become very familiar in psychoanalytic thought – apart perhaps from 'learning from scavenging' which has been little noticed, possibly owing to the group pressure to produce supposedly original ideas. This epistemological dimension is termed the 'most important' for the purpose of this study, yet only comes into proper relief when partnered with its psychoanalytical basis – the personality organisation of the individual. This may be in flux between adult and infantile states of mind: the adult state being that which is capable of learning from experience, while the infantile states learn through projective identification and mimicry.

The various modes of learning are respectively encouraged or discouraged by various types of family organisation. For each mode of individual learning, from the regressive to the most progressive, has its parallel in the wider circles of family and community. At the regressed end of the spectrum are the basic assumption groups and gang-style families; at the progressive end are the work groups and combined-parental families. The types are listed as: the couple family, the matriarchal, patriarchal, gang and reversed families. For groups as well as individuals have a psychological reality associated with a set of values or ethics that are being put into practice.

The 'couple family' has the most psychologically advanced parental ethic, functioning under the aegis of the 'combined object'. This does not refer to an ideal or typical type of external family setup, but describes the roles and functions of the parent figure(s) that mediate between the child and the wider community. Its male–female capacity is defined as containing pain, setting limits and arousing hope: the same as the goal of the psychoanalyst. The couple family has no need of scapegoats or black sheep; it is not cosily barricaded against the badness within, projected outward, since:

> The growth of *all* members of the family, as evidenced by carefully monitored and frequently discussed indicators of physical, social, intellectual and emotional development, is necessary to maintain the sense of security which is intrinsic to the family and is felt to be utterly independent of the community, despite the overall optimistic and benevolent view taken of the natural and social milieu.
>
> ([1986] 2018, p. 187)

Its sense of security is founded on inclusiveness, and this extends beyond the family to the wider world:

> The parental ethic of work and responsibility for the world and its children, human, animal or vegetable, is [the] central preoccupation [of the combined maternal–paternal object] and the source of its joy. Its capacity for loving companionship in sexuality generates the family, while its capacity for friendly co-operation makes the work-group (Bion) possible. It begins to form early in childhood.
>
> (Meltzer & Harris [1976] 2013, p. 29)

The genuinely secure family atmosphere has a sense of potential mobility, however attached to the home or community: it is always ready to move onwards. The progressive function of the family (love, hopefulness, containing pain and thinking) is impelled by a group sense of being presided over by a combined couple – yet the people who perform this function may or may not be the actual parents, and may perform it only temporarily for a specific situation. They may indeed be therapists, family friends or schoolteachers, or any of those transference figures that support the adult state of mind in the child and facilitate his learning from experience.

It may be asked, how can a parental state of mind be maintained, given the natural and inevitable fluctuations of real parents? In a seminar conducted in Italy discussing family dynamics within the culture, Meltzer and Harris discuss what is meant by a good upbringing and focus on the importance of 'interest' in the child, which requires receptivity and reverie:

D.M.: It's all based on unconscious identification. What we seem to come up with is the impression that the main factor in good upbringing is interest in the children. That is different from what we thought twenty years ago in psychoanalytic circles, and that was different from what was thought forty years ago.

M.H.: I would think that that is, in fact, what does break the mould of identification with not-very-good parents sometimes. The mould can be broken. A mother or parents can look at their child, get interested in their child and *also learn from the child.* They learn what the child is like, think about it, and so have their *own* experience. ... [The parents] are both so involved, projecting themselves into the game, that they are not able to stand at a little distance in reverie, thinking about how the child is playing.

(in Negri & Harris [2007] 2018, pp. 176–177)

(The material presented by the observer showed parents being more interested in the toys they had bought for the child, than in the meaning of the child's play.)

The Model, we remember, aims to make describable what is *actually* happening in the child or family or community – not what *appears* to be happening. It looks beneath the titular roles of a prototypal nuclear family (mother, father, children, baby, etc.) and notes instead the masculine or feminine or dependent roles and functions that are actually performed within a family by its members, whatever their number, age or sex:

> It is necessary to put to one side the nominal structure of families in order to describe their real psycho-social arrangement, both with respect to roles (titular) and functions (actual). Taking each member as a human being, unfettered by the preconceptions on stereotype, it is possible in studying a family group to recognize the actual organization of functions and to notice its interaction with the preservation of titular roles.
>
> (Meltzer & Harris [1976], 2013, p. 30)

As is discussed in the matriarchal and patriarchal sections, it is clear that a single parent can include sufficient attributes of the opposite sex to enable a 'combined object' representation to be available to the children. And a baby can perform an adult function for the family as a whole. The 'adult state of mind' is 'no respecter of age' or of external precepts, but is bound to other people through a 'private sharing of the world of objects'.

The opposite is also true: when the adults are overtaken by infantile modes or by forms of negative family existence such as the gang or 'reversed' mode, this leads to a narcissistic or basic assumption grouping based on an ambience of 'lies'. The presiding atmosphere in a family at any time may be: to generate love, to promulgate hate, to promote hope, to sow despair, to contain depressive pain, to emanate persecutory anxiety, to create confusion or to think – depending upon what type of family it is at that period or moment. For the various types of family are not static, and no family is likely to stay within one category, but is liable to move between categories according to the current emotional situation between its members, which can change even when the physical members remain the same.

In conclusion therefore, the Model is designed to enable parents and educators to consider the educational function of the family as distinct from the training needs of the community. And Meltzer observes that despite the modern perception that the 'planetary pull of the family' appears to have fallen to pieces, this does not apply to the psychological reality of the structure of the human mind, which will find its own developmental aids in the outside world, whatever the circumstances:

> We forget that the genetic structure of the baby is something that has been prepared over millions of years and is in no sense chaotic. The speed with which children adapt themselves and learn is evidence of the degree to which development is programmed from limitless past generations. The developmental roots are there, inbuilt.
>
> ([2000a] 2021, p. 110)

The 'gravitational pull' of internal objects is too strong and too ancient to fail to find some correspondence and realisation in the external world. Progress cannot be prescribed but it may be 'assisted from the roots'. Whether it is the standard nuclear family or some other type of care, at parental or social level, the human mind has an inbuilt drive towards development. This is Meltzer's ultimate optimism, like wishing 'good luck' to the next generation of analysts.

Note

1 From an open letter to the Association of Child Psychotherapists, cited in Williams (2010), p. 152.

Key texts

Meltzer, D. ([1978] 2018). *The Kleinian Development*, vol. 3. London: Harris Meltzer Trust.

Meltzer, D., & Harris, M. ([1976] 2013). *The Educational Role of the Family: A Psychoanalytical Model.* London: Harris Meltzer Trust.

Meltzer, D., & Williams, M. H. ([1988] 2018). *The Apprehension of Beauty.* London: Harris Meltzer Trust.

Glossary of Meltzerian concepts

Adhesive identification A concept found in Bick's descriptions of psychic skin and illuminated by work with autistic children, allowing no separation between self and object.

Aesthetic conflict The emotional turbulence experienced in the *presence* of the object, aroused by its mysterious unknown qualities. Love and hate together are resolved by the desire for knowledge.

Aesthetic reciprocity Reciprocity between mother and baby (or equivalent) modulates the turbulence of aesthetic conflict and leads towards understanding.

Claustrum A new view of narcissistic pathology in terms of intrusive identification with the inside of the internal mother: expressed by the phantasy of living in any of three areas with their own characteristics: head–breast, genital and rectal.

Combined object Klein's concept reformulated as the internal fount of creativity and procreative sexuality.

Countertransference dream The state of reverie which is the analyst's response to the patient's dream or phantasy life.

Dismantling A defence used by autistic children to deflect the emotional impact of the object through separating the senses.

Dream-life The theatre for the generating of meaning; continuous in both waking and sleeping states, and merely sampled in psychoanalysis, through attention and observation.

Family types Catalogued in the child in the family in the community as: the couple family, the matriarchal family, the patriarchal family, the gang family and the 'reversed' delinquent family.

Interest An essential reason for doing psychoanalysis, key to therapeutic efficacy.

Learning types Catalogued in the child in the family in the community as: learning from experience, from projective identification, from adhesive identification, from scavenging and from delusion.

Preformed transference Distinguishing the true transference (a *present* relationship) from the preconceptions brought by the analysand (usually owing to previous reading).

Projective and intrusive identification Two types of projective identification are distinguished: the communicative (healthy) and the intrusive (pathological).

Pseudo-maturity A common clinical manifestation of arrested development, the result of living in the head–breast chamber of the Claustrum, intolerant of ignorance.

Psychoanalytic process This has a 'natural history' in five phases – the gathering of the transference, the sorting of geographical confusions, the sorting of zonal confusions, the threshold of the depressive position and the weaning process.

Sexual states Adult and infantile states are differentiated; perversity is differentiated from psychosexual exploration, especially in the case of adolescents. Unconscious phantasy, not physical action, is the key to the meaning of sexuality.

Symbol formation A symbol is a container for meaning created unconsciously by two communicating minds or parts of the mind and finding expression. It is different from a sign which has a pre-existing fixed reference.

Toilet-breast An essential function of the breast as earliest object, the first attribute of the analyst for the patient.

Transference, gathering of The true infantile transference has to be 'gathered' in order for the 'analytic situation' to be established.

Two-dimensionality The result of autistic 'dismantling', resulting in adhesive identification.

Tyranny The sadomasochistic result of living in the rectal chamber of the Claustrum.

Bibliography

For a full Meltzer bibliography see www.harris-meltzer-trust.org.uk

Bick, E. ([1968] 2018). The experience of the skin in early object relations. In: Williams, M. H. (Ed.), *The Tavistock Model: Collected Papers of Martha Harris and Esther Bick*, pp. 139–143. London: Harris Meltzer Trust.

Bion, W. R. (1970). *Attention and Interpretation*. London: Tavistock.

Cassese, S. F. (2002). *An Introduction to the Work of Donald Meltzer*. London: Routledge.

Harris, M. ([1978] 2018). The individual in the group: on learning to work with the psychoanalytical method. In: Williams, M. H. (Ed.), *The Tavistock Model: Collected Papers of Martha Harris and Esther Bick*, pp. 25–42. London: Harris Meltzer Trust.

Harris, M. ([1982] 2018). Growing points in psychoanalysis inspired by the work of Melanie Klein. In: Williams, M. H. (Ed.), *The Tavistock Model: Collected Papers of Martha Harris and Esther Bick*, pp. 63–88. London: Harris Meltzer Trust.

Isaacs, S. (1948). The nature and function of phantasy. *International Journal of Psychoanalysis*, 29: 73–97.

Klein, M. (1963). On the sense of loneliness. In: Jaques E. and Joseph B. (Eds.), *Our Adult World and Other Essays*, pp. 99–116. London: Heinemann.

Meltzer, D. ([1967] 2018). *The Psychoanalytical Process*. London: Harris Meltzer Trust.

Meltzer, D. ([1973] 2018). *Sexual States of Mind*. London: Harris Meltzer Trust.

Meltzer, D. ([1974] 2021). Narcissistic foundation of the erotic transference. In: Williams, M. H. (Ed.), *Selected Papers*, vol. 3, pp. 55–61. London: Harris Meltzer Trust.

Meltzer, D. ([1975] 2018). *Explorations in Autism*. London: Harris Meltzer Trust.

Meltzer, D. ([1976] 2021). Temperature and distance as technical dimensions of interpretation. In: Williams, M. H. (Ed.), *Selected Papers of Donald Meltzer*, vol. 3, pp. 87–98. London: Harris Meltzer Trust.

Meltzer, D. ([1978] 2018). *The Kleinian Development*, 3 vols. London: Harris Meltzer Trust.

Meltzer, D. (1979). Mrs Klein's spatial-theological revolution. www.harris-meltzer-trust.org.uk/pdfs/MeltzerKleinSpatial_PCC.pdf

Meltzer, D. ([1981] 2014). Does Money-Kyrle's concept of misconception have any unique descriptive power? Reprinted in Money-Kyrle, R. (2014). *Man's Picture of his World*, pp. 239–256. London: Harris Meltzer Trust.

Meltzer, D. ([1984] 2018). *Dream Life*. London: Harris Meltzer Trust.

Meltzer, D. ([1986] 2018). *Studies in Extended Metapsychology*. London: Harris Meltzer Trust.

Meltzer. D. ([1989] 2021). Carrying the transference: from Freud to Klein to Bion. In: Williams, M. H. (Ed.), *Selected Papers of Donald Meltzer*, vol. 3, pp. 21–31. London: Harris Meltzer Trust.

Meltzer, D. ([1992] 2018). *The Claustrum*. London: Harris Meltzer Trust.

Meltzer, D. ([1994] 2018). Foreword. In: Negri, R. *The Newborn in the Intensive Care Unit*, pp. xvii–xxi. London: Harris Meltzer Trust.

Meltzer, D. ([1997] 2021). On thought disorders. In: Williams M. H. (Eds.) *Selected Papers*, vol. 2, pp. 73–84. London: Harris Meltzer Trust.

Meltzer, D. ([2000a] 2021). On symbol formation and allegory. In: Williams M. H. (Eds.) *Selected Papers*, vol. 2, pp. 127–137. London: Harris Meltzer Trust.

Meltzer, D. (2000b). A review of my writings. In: Cohen, M., & Hahn, H. (Eds.), *Exploring the Work of Donald Meltzer: A Festschrift*, pp. 1–11. London: Karnac.

Meltzer, D. ([2001a] 2017). Symbols in psychoanalysis and mathematics. In: Touzé, J. (Ed.), *Meltzer in Paris*, p. 213–217. London: Harris Meltzer Trust.

Meltzer, D. ([2001b] 2017). The task of psychoanalysis. In: Touzé, J. (Ed.), *Meltzer in Paris*, pp. 209–212. London: Harris Meltzer Trust.

Meltzer. D. ([2002a] 2021). Invention and discovery. In: Williams, M. H. (Ed.), *Selected Papers of Donald Meltzer*, vol. 2, pp. 167–172. London: Harris Meltzer Trust.

Meltzer. D. ([2002b] 2021). Good luck. In: Williams, M. H. (Ed.), *Selected Papers of Donald Meltzer*, vol. 3, pp. 169–174. London: Harris Meltzer Trust.

Meltzer, D. (2005a). Psychoanalysis acknowledges its poetic forebears and joins the artistic family. In: Williams, M. H. (Ed.), *The Vale of Soulmaking*, pp. xi–xix. London: Karnac.

Meltzer, D. (2005b). 'Thought disorder': a distinct phenomenological category? *British Journal of Psychotherapy*, 21(3): 418–428.

Meltzer, D. (2005c). Creativity and the countertransference. In: Williams, M. H. (Ed.), *The Vale of Soulmaking*, pp. 175–182. London: Karnac.

Meltzer, D., & Harris, M. ([1976] 2013). *The Educational Role of the Family: A Psychoanalytical Model*. London: Harris Meltzer Trust.

Meltzer, D., & Harris, M. ([2011] 2018). *Adolescence: Talks and Papers by Donald Meltzer and Martha Harris*. London: Harris Meltzer Trust.

Meltzer, D., & Williams, M. H. ([1988] 2018). *The Apprehension of Beauty*. London: Harris Meltzer Trust.

Money-Kyrle, R. (1968). Cognitive development. Reprinted in: Money-Kyrle, R. (2014). *Man's Picture of His World*, pp. 209–228. London: Harris Meltzer Trust.

Negri, R. ([1994] 2018). *The Newborn in the Intensive Care Unit*. London: Harris Meltzer Trust.

Negri, R., & Harris, M. ([2007] 2018). *The Story of Infant Development: Observational Work with Martha Harris*. London: Harris Meltzer Trust.

Oelsner, M., & Oelsner, R. (2005). About supervision: an interview with Donald Meltzer. *British Journal of Psychotherapy*, 21(3): 455–461.

Segal, H. (1957). Notes on symbol formation. *International Journal of Psychoanalysis*, 38: 391–397.

Williams, M. H. (2009). An introduction to the work and thinking of Donald Meltzer. www.harris-meltzer-trust.org.uk/pdfs/MeltzerIntro.pdf.

Williams, M. H. (Ed.) ([2010] 2018). *A Meltzer Reader*. London: Harris Meltzer Trust.

Index

Abraham, K. 7, 72
adhesive identification 38–44, 57, 68, 145
adolescence 63–5, 73, 74–6, 79, 96, 143; confusions in 74; obsessional mechanisms in 74
adult sexual state 73, 77–9
aesthetic conflict 18, 38, 45–56, 58–9, 139, 143; of analyst 93, 112; and LHK 100
aesthetic object 42–44, 141; analysis as 88–90, 94, 104, 138; breast as 47; dream as 26, 110; and prenatal life 50–56
aesthetic reciprocity 48, 52, 54, 62
alpha-function 17, 18, 34, 127; and dimensionality 43; in reverse 69, 124; *see also* symbol formation
anxiety 18, 35, 111, 120; and aesthetic object 43, 90; analyst's 86, 94, 109; artist's 140; depressive and persecutory 121, 149; foetal 52; modulation of 92; and thinking 37
artist: creativity of 80, 140; psychoanalyst as 10, 55, 111, 136; relationship to viewer 141–2
autism, infantile 38–44, 127, 130

basic assumption groupings 18, 24, 42, 71, 94, 124; in families 146, 149; internal 61, 126
Bick, E. 2, 34, 38, 40, 129, 134
Bion, W. R., ideas: 15–17, 54, 65, 69, 86, 94, 102, 110, 138; alpha-function 71; attention 23; basic assumptions 42; catastrophic change 46, 52, 89; container–contained 36; emotional links 49, 87, 125–6; exoskeleton 128; Grid 17, 36, 68, 90, 111, 126; intersection with 'O' 79, 135; knowing about 107; language of achievement 123; learning from experience 28; LHK 100; memory and desire 17, 19, 28, 94; the new idea 45; prenatal life 134; projective identification 32; Ps↔D 14, 36, 59, 80, 91; reverie 34, 108; thinking 131, 143; vertices 136
Bremner, J. 38
Breuer, J. 9

Cassirer, E. 24, 28, 119
catastrophic change 17, 37, 47, 52, 89, 94, 112; and 'thing-in-itself' 135–7

Claustrum 33, 57–69; *vs.* container 38; three chambers of 60–68
combined object 34, 35, 71, 131; and creative sexuality 77–81, 147; internal 58, 70, 76; mother as 62; and super-ego-ideal 73; *see also* objects, internal
consciousness, as organ 10, 23, 60, 100, 109, 124
consensuality 41
container-contained 17, 32, 36–8, 40, 67; and analytic process 87–8, 138; *vs.* Claustrum 38; and combined object 70; and the gang 42; internalisation of 19; seminar as 131
countertransference 15, 21, 36, 86, 88, 89, 94, 97, 101, 102–17, 123; as action 92, 126; as dream 92, 106–10; in supervision 131–3; *see also* transference
creativity 63, 79; of analyst 110, 113, 134; of artist 79–80, 139, 140; of dreams 26, 28; of imagination 46; of internal object 58, 71, 77, 79; of memory 56; and sexuality 70–101

death instinct 10, 13, 47, 57, 67, 125
delusional system 68–9, 128
depressive and paranoid-schizoid positions 12, 13, 14, 51, 72, 73, 75, 117, 121, 128, 140; and beauty 47, 50; and catastrophic change 18; Ps↔D oscillation 14, 36, 59, 80, 91; and reparation 28, 78; and weaning 95–100
development, field conception of 15
dismantling 38, 41, 101; *see also* two-dimensionality
dream life 21–30, 100; creativity of 26, 28; and mental growth 27; as presentational form 22; and thinking 130, 131, 137; and unconscious phantasy 11, 24, 70
dreams 18, 114–16: aesthetic theory of 24–7; and children's play 23, 131; countertransference 93, 106–10; interpretation of 111–13, 139; as landmarks 89; poetic diction of 112; and symbol formation 21, 27, 51, 55, 111

epistemophilic instinct *see* knowledge
ethics 18–20, 60, 71, 77, 80; of groups 146; of psychoanalysis 94

family: and adolescents 74; as educator 145; functions of 149; and internal objects 12, 28, 150; types of 146–9; *see also* learning
Freud, S., ideas: 17, 89, 98, 136, 138; body-ego 54; consciousness 124; dualism 126; identification 31; neurophysiological model 8–10; psychic inertia 86; repetition compulsion 105; sexuality 72; superego ideal 70, 73; theory of dreams 22–24; technique 119, 120; transference 9, 102, 106; two principles 16

Grid (Bion's) 17, 18, 38, 126; Negative 18, 68, 90

Harris, M. 2, 9, 34, 35, 42, 129, 131, 134, 138, 144, 147
Hoxter, S. 38

identification, types of 31–35: *see also* adhesive identification; introjective identification; projective identification
identity, sense of 58, 72, 74, 77, 79

infantile parts/states 31, 34, 58, 60, 78, 98, 106, 126, 140, 146; and sexuality 61, 72–74
infantile transference 12, 95, 109, 123, 127
infant observation 35, 71, 129, 134
inner world 1, 3, 23, 24, 145; of child 46, 48; and claustrophobia 68; concreteness of 60; as spatial 11–15
integration 13, 74, 77, 78, 98, 125, 127, 140; and combined object 79
interest 47–50
introjective identification 33–35, 75, 77, 97, 99, 100
intrusive identification *see* projective identification
invention v. discovery 80, 136
Isaacs, S. 23

Kant, I. 7, 134
Klein, M., ideas: analytic situation 95; combined object 71, 136; depressive position 78; epistemophilic instinct 16, 42; first post-Kleinian 15; the positions 51; reparation 78, 125; spatial model 11–15, 23, 37, 58, 139; schizoid mechanisms 58, 106; splitting and idealisation 40, 127
knowledge, search for 16, 19, 34, 36, 62, 94: avoidance of 41, 59, 91, 106; and education 80, 143; and epistemophilic instinct 12, 16, 4, 3, 48; knowing about 107; and LHK 18, 49, 59, 100, 125; *see also* learning, types of

Langer, S. 24, 47, 119
language: of achievement 52, 123; in dreams 26, 29, 113, 130; functions of 25, 32, 110, 120; music of 122; non-verbal 48, 135, 138; origins of 33, 123; preverbal modes 32, 52, 122, 123; and symbol formation 28, 127; of unconscious phantasy; *see also* symbol formation
learning, types of 145; from experience 17, 28, 34, 36, 49, 55, 71, 129, 143; and adult state of mind 146; the analyst's 92; in the family 144; through the object 79; v. knowing about 107; *see also* knowledge, search for
LHK and minus LHK 18, 49, 66; and aesthetic conflict 100

Maizels, N. 120
memory and desire 17, 19, 28, 94
memory as structure 55
mindlessness 39, 126
misconception 68, 70, 113–117
Money-Kyrle, R. 1, 11, 18–20, 68, 70; on misconception 71, 77, 113–16
mother-baby relationship 8, 11, 17, 32, 35, 43, 55, 122, 148; aesthetic reciprocity of 48; defences in 57, 61; mismatch in 114; in psychoanalysis 36, 114; and self-knowledge 50
music (in psychoanalysis) *see* language, music of

negative capability 49
Negri, R. 54

objects, internal 4, 12, 13, 28, 58, 65, 96, 99; conversation with 85, 87, 101, 104, 123; creativity of 77; as gods 18–20, 102, 136, 139; inside of 33, 60–61, 67; integration of 79, 140; *see also* combined object

observation, in psychoanalysis 3, 11, 23, 38, 55, 85, 92, 101, 114, 121, 124, 144; and countertransference dream 107–10; *see also* infant observation
Oedipus complex 31, 74, 96, 99
Oelsner, M., & Oelsner, R. 131

paranoid-schizoid *see* depressive and paranoid-schizoid positions
part-objects 2, 11, 23, 95, 97, 109 *see also* objects, internal
perversions and addictions 66, 72, 76–77, 97
phantasy 11, 13, 23, 25, 32, 64, 78, 97; of dead babies 77; and external/internal object 58; and mother's body 31, 61; of parental intercourse 70; and projective identification 32, 58; theatre of 23, 123; as trial action 40; *see also* dreams
post-Kleinian *see* psychoanalytic models, post-Kleinian
preconception 70, 77, 116, 137, 148; of mother-as-the-world 61
prenatal life 50–56, 123, 134
preverbal communication *see* language, preverbal modes
projective identification 31–33, 41, 58, 60, 68, 76, 114, 120, 124; and intrusive 32, 57, 61, 95, 124; Klein's paper 106; learning from 146
protomental states 17, 26, 41–42, 43, 127, 143
pseudo-maturity 58, 63
psychic reality 4, 15, 23, 33, 61, 63, 65, 87, 98; denial of 12, 24, 43, 61, 117; in family life 144; of unborn children 75
psychoanalytic models: neurophysiological 8; structural 10; geographic/spatial 11; and method 85, 89, 102, 111, 118, 138; post-Kleinian 15–20, 35–37, 49, 79, 88; theological 8, 12, 136
psychoanalytic process 95; as aesthetic 45, 90, 119, 139; as corrective 13; setting for 37; 91–94, 98, 105, 108, 119–20, 123, 131; natural history 94–101; weaning 99–101
psychoanalysis: as art-science 3, 9, 55, 80, 111, 136; as collaborative investigation 9, 113; method of 3, 7, 9, 19, 72, 85, 87, 88, 94; as thing-in-itself 89, 104, 135–43; as work group 18, 89, 122, 129, 138; *see also* transference
psychoanalyst 36, 80, 85–100; as artist 123; countertransference problems 108; language 123; and preformed transference 104–5; and the setting 108; and technique 91, 109, 118, 123–8; temperature and distance 116, 118, 120; and transference 106–7; as thinker 107, 127, 130; as visitor to Claustrum 124, 128

sadomasochism 60, 64, 73, 76, 141
Segal, H. 24, 27, 32, 58
separation 41, 51, 73, 87, 96, 99, 124; rhythm of 91; *see also* adhesive identification
sermonising 79, 142
sexuality: adolescent 74; adult 76–81; infantile 72–6; and internal objects 58, 79, 150; revised theory 71
Sharpe, E. F. 22, 26, 111
splitting: and idealisation 33, 40; and integration 13, 78, 79, 98, 125, 140; and toilet-breast 95
Stokes, A. 90, 139, 140–42
sublimation 11, 77, 78, 139

Sullivan, H. S. 41
supervision 87, 93, 118, 129–133
surprise 9, 51, 86, 102, 105
symbol formation 17, 19, 24–30, 37, 43, 106, 108, 127, 130; and aesthetic conflict 49; *v.* allegory 28; and analytic setting 135–8; artist's 80, 139; and dreams 22, 26–7, 110; *v.* signs 21; locus of 62; origins of 55; preverbal 53; problems of 42, 51, 64, 88; *see also* alpha-function

Tavistock Clinic 7, 144
technical problems *see* psychoanalyst, and technique
temperature and distance *see* psychoanalyst, temperature and distance
termination/weaning *see* psychoanalytic process, weaning
thinking 15–17, 103, 107, 124, 130, 136; attacks on 18, 59, 125; and emotional experiences 16; mother's 35, 71; origins of 18, 37; pseudo- 24; *v.* protomental 127, 143; as work group 18, 89, 122, 129, 138
Thompson, D. W. 138
toilet-breast 95, 97 *see also* part-objects
transference 13–15, 33, 35, 85, 95, 99, 102–7, 120; and container–contained 88; Freud's discovery 7; gathering of 94; new understanding of 31, 86; and observation 55; perversion of 77; preformed 95, 104–7, 127; relinquishment of 101; *see also* countertransference
truth, analytic 16, 18, 19, 49, 87, 90, 92, 102–3, 108; degradation of 66, 71, 98, 144–5; of dreams 24, 112
two-dimensionality 38–43; and three-dimensionality 127
tyranny 58, 59, 65, 76 *see also* Claustrum

Weddell, D. 38
Whitehead, A. N. 24, 143
Williams, M. H. 139
Winnicott, D. 47
Wittenberg, I. 38

Printed in Great Britain
by Amazon